How to Resolve Conflict in Organizations

This is a comprehensive guide using People Models to understand and resolve conflict at different levels of the organization. It starts at the inter-organizational level explaining conflict between organizations that are involved in mergers and acquisitions. It looks at this kind of conflict not from the point of view of a business and economic rationale but from the point of view of there being a relationship between the two organizations. Here, this relationship is described by a People Model which outlines three different relationship types. In the subsequent chapters we look at the organizational level; first at structural conflict and then at team conflict. In each chapter there is a People Model to explain and resolve conflict. Structural conflict is explained by the Myers Briggs Type Indicator (MBTI) and team conflict is explained by the Schutz model of Inclusion, Control and Openness. In the next chapter the conflict is explained in terms of Gestalt psychology and looks at interpersonal conflict. Carl Jung is then used to explore inner conflict; followed by a chapter on life conflict exploring conflict in terms of how you live a life. The final chapter is focused on the applications of the People Models analysing Donald Trump and Tony Blair.

Following through the entire book is a step-by-step procedure called a People Procedure, which is contrasted with a Business Procedure. The former guides you through a process to unravel and resolve conflict.

Annamaria Garden is an independent organizational consultant. She has over 20 years' experience in the field of organizational and personal change and has experience running her own self-employed consulting and facilitation practice in London, gaining a reputation for being creative, leading edge and dependable. She has a PhD from the Massachusetts Institute of Technology (Boston).

How to Resolve Conflict in Organizations

How to Resolve Conflict in Organizations

The Power of People Models and Procedure

Annamaria Garden

LONDON AND NEW YORK

First published 2018
by Routledge
2 Park Square, Milton Park, Abingdon, Oxon OX14 4RN

and by Routledge
711 Third Avenue, New York, NY 10017

Routledge is an imprint of the Taylor & Francis Group, an informa business

© 2018 Annamaria Garden

The right of Annamaria Garden to be identified as author of this work has been asserted by her in accordance with sections 77 and 78 of the Copyright, Designs and Patents Act 1988.

All rights reserved. The purchase of this copyright material confers the right on the purchasing institution to photocopy pages which bear the photocopy icon and copyright line at the bottom of the page. No other parts of this book may be reprinted or reproduced or utilized in any form or by any electronic, mechanical, or other means, now known or hereafter invented, including photocopying and recording, or in any information storage or retrieval system, without permission in writing from the publishers.

Trademark notice: Product or corporate names may be trademarks or registered trademarks, and are used only for identification and explanation without intent to infringe.

British Library Cataloguing-in-Publication Data
A catalogue record for this book is available from the British Library

Library of Congress Cataloging-in-Publication Data
Names: Garden, Anna-Maria, author.
Title: How to resolve conflict in organizations : the power of people models and procedure / Annamaria Garden.
Description: 1 Edition. | New York : Routledge, 2018.
Identifiers: LCCN 2018002623 | ISBN 9780815383321 (hardback) |
ISBN 9780815383338 (pbk.) | ISBN 9781351206112 (eBook)
Subjects: LCSH: Conflict management.
Classification: LCC HD42 .G337 2018 | DDC 658.3/145–dc23
LC record available at https://lccn.loc.gov/2018002623

ISBN: 978-0-8153-8332-1 (hbk)
ISBN: 978-0-8153-8333-8 (pbk)
ISBN: 978-1-351-20611-2 (ebk)

Typeset in Times New Roman
by Wearset Ltd, Boldon, Tyne and Wear
Printed and bound by CPI Group (UK) Ltd, Croydon, CR0 4YY

Contents

List of figures	ix
List of tables	x
List of checklists	xii
List of commentaries	xiii
Acknowledgements	xiv

Introduction	1

1 People Models and People Procedure   4

Getting the angels to win 4
Key points in this chapter 4
Business language and people language 5
People Models 6
Conflict 6
Other models of conflict resolution 6
Not fitting the traditional mould 7
People Procedure 8
Stopping the Department working on Sunday 9
The six different People Models 10
Values 13
Conclusion 14
Exercises 14

2 Relationships between organizations   16

The computer users' groups 16
Key points in this chapter 17
M&As: business language 17
An acquisition that is on tenterhooks 18
Research backs up the acquiring company's approach 19
Factors associated with job excitement 19

vi *Contents*

The People Procedure applied to the acquisition 19
The People Model: Partner–Ally–Friend 20
Conflicts between the two 21
Conflict in the voluntary sector 23
Negotiating to Yes 24
*Four organizations merge into one: the case of the public
   sector 25*
Conclusion 28
*Case studies: Sir Alex Ferguson, Angela Merkel,
   Richard Branson 29*
Exercises 30
Checklist 2.1 Assessing Partner–Ally–Friend 31

3   Conflict within organizations – structure 34
A classic framework 34
Key points in this chapter 34
Functional or lateral conflict 34
The Administration and Marketing departments 35
The People Model: the MBTI 35
Cautions around using the MBTI 40
Bureaucratic conflict 41
The retail company 41
Bargaining conflict 45
Annihilating HR 45
Moving on 48
Conclusion 48
Case study: Theresa May, British PM 49
Exercises 50
*Checklist 3.1 The dynamic of type in the organization as a
   whole 51*
*Checklist 3.2 Where do we need to develop as an
   organization? 53*

4   Conflict within organizations – teams 55
The importance of teams 55
Key points in this chapter 56
The Executive Committee who never met 56
The People Model: Inclusion–Control–Openness 57
Humming as a team 59
General theory of the People Model 59
Research on teams 62
Digging deeper into the Inclusion–Control–Openness theory 63
The other Executive Committee 66

Contents vii

Determining the main dimension 67
Conclusion 68
Case study: Sir Alex Ferguson 69
Exercises 71
Checklist 4.1 Connoisseur or Populist 72
Checklist 4.2 Juggler or Boss 73
Checklist 4.3 Professional or Attractor 74
Checklist 4.4 How well does your organization meet Inclusion issues? 75
Checklist 4.5 How well does your organization meet Control issues? 76
Checklist 4.6 How well does your organization meet Openness issues? 77

5 Interpersonal conflict 79

Projection 79
Key points in this chapter 79
Other defence mechanisms 80
Up the Swiss Alps 82
Feedback from the troops 83
The Gestalt Cycle of Experience 84
Resistance to the Cycle of Experience 85
Empowered leadership 86
Other interruptions in the Cycle of Experience 87
Different modes of dealing with conflict 89
Conclusion 92
Case study: Flight Centre or FCTG 93
Exercises 94
Checklist 5.1 The Cycle Of Experience – Individual 95
Checklist 5.2 The Cycle of Experience – Organization 96

6 Inner conflicts 98

Detecting inner conflict 98
Key points in this chapter 98
The case of the cat 99
The People Model: Carl Jung 99
Back to the boss 102
Balance between conscious and unconscious 102
Burnout 103
Enantiadromia 105
The boss' protégée 106
Two Introverted Feeling types 108
Individuation 110

viii *Contents*

Conclusion 111
Case study: Richard Branson 112
Exercises 112
Checklist 6.1 Development profile 114

7 Life conflicts – individual 116

The effective MD: the power of personality 116
Key points in this chapter 116
The People Procedure: putting three states together 117
The People Model: Life Conflicts 117
Existence 117
Susan Wojcicki, CEO of YouTube 119
Elevation 120
Jeremy Moon, CEO of Icebreaker 121
Efficacy 121
Sadiq Khan, Mayor of London 123
Becoming more good humoured 123
Monitoring the three states 125
Organizations and conflict 126
Conclusion 126
Case study: Steve Jobs 127
Exercises 129
Checklist 7.4 Existence in the organization 129
Checklist 7.5 Elevation in the organization 130
Checklist 7.6 Efficacy in the organization 131

8 Applying the People Models 132

Getting an overview 132
Key points in this chapter 132
Culturally preferred styles 133
Applying a procedure 134
Applying the People Models: politicians 135
Barack Obama 135
Hillary Clinton 137
President Trump 139
ESTP 144
Tony Blair 145
Conclusion 150
Exercises 150

Index 151

Figures

4.1	Connoisseur and Populist	64
4.2	Juggler and Boss	65
4.3	Professional and Attractor	66
6.1	Jungian map of the psyche	100
7.1	Three modes of conflict	124

Tables

1.1	Key points in this chapter	5
1.2	Demons and angels in this book	5
1.3	Meta-theoretical traditions for conflict	7
1.4	The People Procedure	9
1.5	Differing contributions of the six models	13
1.6	Summary of the book	13
2.1	Key points in this chapter	17
2.2	Partners and Allies	21
2.3	Partners and Friends	22
2.4	Friends and Allies	22
2.5	Underlying needs of relationship types	27
3.1	Key points in this chapter	35
3.2	Basic descriptors of the MBTI dimensions	37
3.3	The MBTI of the Administration and Marketing departments	38
3.4	The MBTI of the Administration and Marketing Managers	39
3.5	The MBTI profile of the RMs and their senior managers	42
3.6	Underlying needs in the relationship	44
3.7	Numbers of type out of 60 possible	46
4.1	Key points in this chapter	56
4.2	General theory of Inclusion–Control–Openness	59
4.3	Underlying needs and feelings of the three dimensions	61
4.4	Core issues for each dimension	62
4.5	Connoisseur and Populist	63
4.6	Juggler and Boss	64
4.7	Professional and Attractor	65
4.8	The main dimension for an organization	67
5.1	Key points in this chapter	80
5.2	Defence mechanisms involved in interpersonal conflict	81
5.3	Resistance to the Cycle of Experience	85
5.4	The two Directors	88
5.5	Provocative and evocative modes of influence	89
6.1	Key points in this chapter	98
6.2	Jung's psychological types	101

Tables xi

6.3	Over-used functions	104
6.4	Emotional demands and mental demands	106
6.5	A tale of two Introverted Feeling types	108
6.6	Inner conflict of two Introverted Feeling types	110
7.1	Key points in this chapter	116
7.2	How you feel in the presence or absence of life conflict	125
7.3	The husband and wife team	125
8.1	Key points in this chapter	132
8.2	Culturally preferred styles in the Western world	133
8.3	Stable and excess Extraversion and Introversion	141
8.4	Conflict arising from an inappropriate response	149

Checklists

2.1	Assessing Partner–Ally–Friend	31
3.1	The dynamic of type in the organization as a whole	51
3.2	Where do we need to develop as an organization?	53
4.1	Connoisseur or Populist	72
4.2	Juggler or Boss	73
4.3	Professional or Attractor	74
4.4	How well does your organization meet Inclusion issues?	75
4.5	How well does your organization meet Control issues?	76
4.6	How well does your organization meet Openness issues?	77
5.1	The Cycle of Experience – Individual	95
5.2	The Cycle of Experience – Organization	96
6.1	Development profile	114
7.1	Existence in the individual	118
7.2	Elevation in the individual	120
7.3	Efficacy in the individual	122
7.4	Existence in the organization	129
7.5	Elevation in the organization	130
7.6	Efficacy in the organization	131

Commentaries

1.1	The People Procedure applied to Administration and Marketing	11
3.1	Theresa May and the MBTI	49
4.1	Sir Alex Ferguson: Connoisseur not Populist	69
4.2	Sir Alex Ferguson: Boss not Juggler	70
4.3	Sir Alex Ferguson: Attractor not Professional	71
6.1	Richard Branson	112
7.1	Susan Wojcicki	119
7.2	Jeremy Moon	121
7.3	Sadiq Khan	123
7.4	Steve Jobs: Existence	127
7.5	Steve Jobs: Elevation	128
7.6	Steve Jobs: Efficacy	128
8.1	Extract from Obama's speeches	136
8.2	Trump: the Ally	140
8.3	Trump on Extraversion: Introversion	141
8.4	Trump on Sensing: Intuition	142
8.5	Trump on Thinking: Feeling	143
8.6	Trump on the media	143
8.7	Trump on Judging: Perceiving	144
8.8	Trump – Populist, Boss, Attractor	146
8.9	Tony Blair's Professional and Attractor	147
8.10	Blair and the Chilcot inquiry	149

Acknowledgements

The illustrations for Figures 4.1, 4.2, 4.3, 6.1 and 7.1 have been kindly and expertly done by Neil White. Excerpts by Susan Wojcicki and Sadiq Khan have been reproduced with permission from *The Economist* while an interview on Jeremy Moon is reproduced with permission from the *NZ Herald*.

Introduction

When I look broadly at what I do as an organizational consultant, I realize that my focus is often that of conflict between and within organizations and that over 50 per cent of what I do is to deal with 'people' conflict. This is the substance of my consulting work even if it is not labelled as such. Conflict is everywhere – in the relationship between a Finance Director and his direct report; in the strategic choices among the members of an executive committee; the appalling team behaviour in another executive committee; in the stand-off between HR and the 'business' that so often occurs; in an acquisition. I have been involved in all of these issues and hundreds more. People didn't understand each other, didn't like each other and there were recurring fights about the business issues.

The resolution between organizations, within organizations, between people is often to look at conflicted *relationships*. For this, we need People Models to break through the heavy emphasis on business models and business language. Therefore, in each chapter in this book there is a different People Model addressing conflict at different levels in the organization (individual, team, structure, for example).

Years ago, I wrote out a model to aid organizations involved in mergers or acquisitions (M&A). This is one area where there is often a great deal of people conflict. In practice, M&As focus on the technical or business aspects including strategy, financing, IT and information systems in general. Some look also to cultural compatibility or incompatibility. The model I created was one that focused on the relationship(s) between the two organizations in the same sense that we have relationships between two people. Much of the conflict within M&As stems from the fact that the organizations have different implicit assumptions about the nature of the relationship that should characterize the two. (In my People Model I have three relationship types: Partner or Ally or Friend. These are described in Chapter 2.)

For example, I consulted once to a UK company who had made a disastrous acquisition in the USA. The acquired company was smaller, successful with a broad spread of distribution channels. They had a comparable range of products. Because of the overlaps in the business, they expected and achieved some redundancies and some resignations. The animosity between them was extreme, however, shouting at each other at odd times. The famed distribution channels

2 Introduction

were not as marvellous as my client expected. While the business factors involved in this acquisition were not wonderful, the relationship between the two was even worse. A manager in the client described their approach to me: they had taken no notice of the people factors and no notice of the relationship. As a result they got no cooperation from the acquired company who sometimes did what they could, covertly, to scupper the success of the enterprise. As my client was larger than the acquired company, they did what they could to walk all over them. They didn't *have* to act this way but, operating with a business model and without a relationship model, it was almost inevitable that they did. (They were both Allies.) Years later, my client had learnt a few lessons from this. They were big enough to look at themselves in the mirror and say: "We did that wrong. We mangled them." However, they did not know how to get out of the habit. If they worked only off business models they would fail again. What they needed was a relationship focus.

Two people locked in conflict exhibit a different scenario and demand for help. For example, in one client they amalgamated the structure dealing with IT and Administration under one person. They selected an IT manager to fill this role. He reported to a Finance Director (the reason why they did this has more to do with his personality and the reach of his role rather than anything else). The incumbent of the IT role was relatively new and a former special forces soldier. He was tough. The Finance Director was a former accountant from one of the large accountancy firms. They hated each other. They were at constant loggerheads. The Finance Director frightened everyone and expected his direct reports to jump when he said he wanted anything. The special forces man didn't jump (when expected to). He was, however, quite put out by the Finance Director. One technical problem was that he was too slow at fulfilling job requirements, as seen in the eyes of the Finance Director. That was the business source of the conflict. If you take a people-approach, you have an entirely different problem. This was that it was a case of bullying so extreme that he even unnerved a former special forces soldier. The Finance Director was a bully. My intervention stemmed at this latter framing of events not at a business framing of events, which avoided the real issue. The solution was to have me sit in the middle of both and moderate the real interpersonal conflict, which I did. Subsequently, it was to give them both a hefty piece of feedback: to the Finance Director who was all over the map; to the IT manager who was playing victim.

The models I use to resolve these conflicts and others are, along with the Partner–Ally–Friend one, the substance of this book. These are the Inclusion–Control–Openness approach derived from Will Schutz (1984); the Myers Briggs Type Indicator (Myers *et al.* 2009) and Carl Jung theories (1959, 1960, 1966, 1971); a Gestalt model (Nevis, 2001) that has as its catalyst being taught by Professor Ed Nevis at MIT where I was a PhD student with him; a model of life conflicts, one on inner conflict; and, finally, a chapter on applying the six models which focuses on Donald Trump. In each chapter, my priority is to increase the understanding of the conflict as well as to resolve it.

It is also a fix-it book. We need a tool box of human things. One tool in the book, for example, is a People Procedure which I use in each chapter. This sets out the list of questions/issues you should address in order to deal with conflict in a human system. The Procedure stays the same throughout the book, till it becomes second nature.

Most books in this field deal either with political or with interpersonal conflict only. There is space in the market for a book aimed at organizations, managers and business students that is part how-to and part theoretical with some research thrown in that looks at organizations as a whole as well as teams and individuals.

References

Jung, C. G. (1959). *The archetypes and the collective unconscious.* In the Collected Works of C. G. Jung (vol. 9). Part 1. London, UK. Routledge & Kegan Paul.

Jung, C. G. (1960). *The structure and dynamics of the psyche.* In the Collected Works of C. G. Jung (vol. 7). Bollinger Series, Princeton, NJ. Princeton University Press.

Jung, C. G. (1966). *Two essays on analytical psychology.* In the Collected Works of C. G. Jung (vol. 17). Bollinger Series, Princeton, NJ. Princeton University Press.

Jung, C. G. (1971). *Psychological types.* In the Collected Works of C. G. Jung (vol. 16). Bollinger series, Princeton, NJ. Princeton University Press.

Myers, I. B., McCaulley, M. H., Quenk, N. L. and Hammer, A. C. (2009). *MBTI Manual,* 3rd ed. Mountain View, CA. CPP Inc.

Nevis, E. (2001). *Organizational consulting: a Gestalt approach.* Cambridge, MA. Gestalt Press.

Schutz, W. (1984). *The truth option.* Berkeley, CA. Ten Speed Press.

1 People Models and People Procedure

Getting the angels to win

Freud was famous for approaching social conflict as an expression of forces "deeply ingrained within the individual. So deeply ingrained are they that it is common to refer to them as basic instincts. For Freud, human conflict fed on the innate aggressive drive lying within us all" (Schellenberg, 1996, p. 42). Pinker (2015) describes and rejects the same phenomenon as the Hydraulic Theory of Violence: that humans "harbour an inner drive toward aggression ... which builds up inside us and must periodically be discharged" (p. 373).

Pinker also describes the fact that, in his view, humans get the better of this Hydraulic Theory in practice. He describes five inner demons that lead to conflict and four better angels that rescue us from it. Pinker explains the demons' psychological systems that differ in their triggers: one is predatory or instrumental violence

> deployed as a practical means to an end. Dominance is the urge for authority, prestige, glory, and power.... Revenge fuels the moralistic urge toward retribution.... Sadism is pleasure taken in another's suffering. And ideology is a shared belief system ... that justifies unlimited violence in pursuit of unlimited good.
>
> (Pinker, 2015 p. 373)

However, there are also four better angels. "Humans ... come equipped with motives that can orient them away from [aggression] and toward cooperation and altruism. Empathy ... a moral sense ... the faculty of reason" (Pinker, 2015, p. 373). In addition, humans have evolved to become less violent or aggressive. In other words, the angels win.

In this book, instead of these four angels, the same intent that propels forces for good to exist we will find as we follow the People Procedure and People Models that resolve conflict. The demons and angels here are quite different from Pinker's but help us get to the same place: the angels win.

Key points in this chapter

Key points in this chapter are illustrated in Table 1.1.

Table 1.1 Key points in this chapter

- Getting the angels to win
- Key points in this chapter
- Business language and people language
- People Models
- Conflict
- Other models of conflict resolution
- Not fitting the traditional mould
- People Procedure
- Stopping the Department working on Sunday
- The six different People Models
- Values
- Conclusion
- Exercises

Business language and people language

The approach to conflict that I take in this book is based on personal experience. It posits a clear distinction between business thinking and people thinking. The former I learnt on my MBA at Cranfield School of Management, UK, and is what I call my 'business language'. Prior to the MBA, I was an economist working in the Treasury in New Zealand and in the UK. However, I turned from that largely because I didn't believe in it, especially the assumption of economic rationality. At Cranfield, I was looking to switch careers. There, I discovered Organizational Behaviour which was the subject I most wanted to read about and spend time on. Once I had figured this, I proceeded to switch careers at the Massachusetts Institute of Technology (MIT) doing my PhD in Organizational Studies. People thinking and people language came on my PhD where I was trained in what I call People Models as well as consulting by Professor Ed Schein, Professor Dick Beckhard, Professor Ed Nevis and Professor Lotte Bailyn. The PhD language won and, in this book, I contrast the two languages with an eye to the People Models winning the contest. Table 1.2 illustrates.

Table 1.2 Demons and angels in this book

Demons	Angels
• Business focus exclusively or primarily	• Focus on people and relationships
• Focus on power, resources, size to justify differential behaviour	• Honourable behaviour and solution; an assumption of equality
• Try to trick the other person/organization	• Confrontation and directness between people
• 'Get the better of' the other person	• Understand the other person
• Act even if you don't understand events	• Psychological intelligence for what is going on; comprehension of events

People Models

Conflict exists everywhere in organizations; from interpersonal dynamics to massive disagreements between organizations. I use People Models to look at conflict because people are usually standing out in the middle of it. There is no one right way to understand or to resolve it. Because of this, this book describes six ways (or People Models) not one way. One of these models might work for you or your organization and the others might not. Or, all might work.

Organizations are full of human beings functioning as human beings not business machines, so we need theories and models that are based on this fact not models that are technical or business-like. To understand conflict we need to understand why people do things. We need also frameworks that can assess conflict at an interpersonal level, as well as for a team, a Division or even the whole organization. These different levels are what this book is about.

Reasons to read this book:

- It helps me deal with people issues.
- It helps me understand the organization, team or individual.
- It is constructive.
- It is hands-on rather than being analytical.
- It gives me six People Models – tools I can apply.
- It gives me examples of applying the People Models.
- It gives me a People Procedure – another tool.
- It is psychological, but doesn't require navel-gazing.

Conflict

Conflict exists when there is some argument, or disagreement between interested parties. The *Concise Oxford Dictionary* defines it as "a serious disagreement or argument, typically a protracted one". It is noise in the system that we do not want. It is a difference that creates tension, not simply a difference per se. Conflict would arise only when there is an issue around positions; where there is some emotion or affect, some angst. It arises also when there is the need for a united front or view and this does not exist. Resolution means that the parties agree to proceed down a particular path. There needn't be 100 per cent agreement to be able to do this.

Different organizations have a higher tolerance for conflict. In some, you are metaphorically walking on eggshells when interacting with people, and in others boldly slamming doors and confronting people.

Other models of conflict resolution

What do academics have to say about conflict? How do they approach it? They do so in a way that is different from my framework. However, here is a brief section describing some alternatives. As Morrill and Rudes (2010) write

People Models and People Procedure   7

Two meta-theoretical traditions mark research on conflict resolution in organizations: the **rationalist** tradition which portrays organizations as goal-directed collectivities and conflict … as a threat to efficiency and performance; and the **cultural** tradition, which portrays organizations as normative [i.e. value-based] collectivities constituted by ongoing social interaction, interpretive dynamics, and institutional environments, and emphasizes the interplay of law and social inequalities in interpersonal and collective organizational conflict resolution. Within those traditions we distinguish between structural and processual styles.

(p. 627)

Table 1.3 illustrates this.

The structural-rational approaches are those that have dominated the study of conflict in organizations. Within this framework, conflict endangers efficiency. It emphasizes engineering and design solutions. The processual-rationalist approach focuses "on the techniques and strategies of negotiation and bargaining" (p. 628).

The major shift has been to the cultural tradition which has gained momentum in recent years, partly because of the post-bureaucratic organizational forms that differ from the bureaucratic forms people are used to. The structural-cultural approach emphasizes the social construction of meaning and forms in organizations. The cultural processual approach explores "interpersonal dynamics, discourse, and collective action" (p. 628).

Not fitting the traditional mould

My own models do not fit any of the above traditions. Here are some of the reasons why; what makes my approach distinctive.

1   As already stated, one contribution of this book is to mix levels. The People Models can be applied inside the individual as well as across organizations.

It is common to assume that the psychological discipline is relevant to the **individual** only. The famous Morton Deutch (2015, p. 72) says the

Table 1.3 Meta-theoretical traditions for conflict

Structural/rational	• Frederick Taylor	• Efficiency, performance, opposed interests
Processual/rational	• Roger Fisher and William Ury; Walton and McKersie	• Bargaining, negotiating, problem solving, strategic choices, distributed and integrative bargaining
Structural/cultural	• Selznick	• Legalization of organizations, formal and informal relations, sociocultural contexts
Processual/cultural	• Barley, Dalton, Kolb	• Everyday social interaction and discourse, behind the scenes, situational meanings

8 *People Models and People Procedure*

"psychological mode explains such phenomena ... in terms of the perceptions, beliefs, values, ideology, motivations and other psychological states and characteristics that individual men and women have acquired".

Many of the models I use are inspired and originate from psychology. However, my use of them is very different from the way psychology is usually applied as per Deutch above. It is thinking of the organization in these different ways that is useful.

2   Another difference with my approach is that it is applied to every aspect of the organization; feelings as well as strategies. Morale as well as mergers. Social and political events as well as psychological.

3   The models are characterized by, for the most part, being non-evaluative. Few of them dictate a solution that blames one party. Instead, they open up the agenda and create understanding of all parties.

4   The six models dig deep; they always examine what is underneath the surface behaviour.

The point of the six People Models:

- They tell me things that are hard to decipher.
- They force me to be constructive.
- They enable me to understand and not judge the other parties.
- They dig deep so solutions are sustainable.
- They give me a starting point.

People Procedure

In addition to the six People Models (which are summarized later in what follows), there is a People Procedure applied in each chapter (the same one in each). The one I use is developed from my consulting work around conflict. It asks questions that are related to people not the business and these are subtly different from the types of questions I would ask if trained only in my MBA. For illustration, in Table 1.4, on the left hand side are the 'business language' questions, steps that would typically be posed during resolution of conflict in business. On the right hand side are the questions that you ask in a People Procedure. You start with a simple diagnostic stance and then answer the question, in your own mind, what the People Model says about what is going on.

The next step is imperative. If all you do is this you have half solved the conflict. This is to establish that all parties are equal no matter their size, wealth etc. They all have an equal voice, say, contribution. They each have an equally valid way to resolve the conflict. They each need to be treated with respect and treated honourably. This may sound wholly unreasonable. However, as you will see in the examples throughout the book, it is a necessary but not sufficient condition for success in resolving conflict.

Next, you decipher their underlying needs (not the 'causes' of the conflict). This is followed by working out the dominant theme of the discussion(s) so far

People Models and People Procedure 9

Table 1.4 The People Procedure

Business Procedure	People Procedure
What is **going** on?	What is **going** on?
What are their respective **positions**?	What does the **People Model** say? Choose one of the six People Models
Do they want a **proportionate** solution (based on power, resources, size etc.)	Do they want an **equal** solution? (each party being treated equally)
What are the **causes** of these issues?	What are the **underlying needs** of the two parties?
What is the **impact** of A on B and vice versa?	What is the **dominant theme** of the whole discussion?
What are the **potential** solutions?	Do the parties *want* to get to a solution?
What is **the best** solution?	What is the **resolution**?

(rather than look at the impact of the parties on each other). The next step is also very important. It is to discern with a psychological eye whether or not the parties really and truly want to get to a solution. Finally, you are at the point of determining what the resolution is.

You use this People Procedure when you want to concentrate on the people not the business. Table 1.4 illustrates this. The anecdote that follows illustrates how to use it in general (albeit without a People Model at this stage since we have yet to explore them).

Stopping the Department working on Sunday

I was in a meeting with the Administration Manager of a client when he exploded with the complaint that the Marketing Department would give them only 24 hours' notice of their required mailings (of the company's brochures). Administration needed three days' notice. The delay gave the Administration Manager a headache with his staff who occasionally had come in on the weekend without pay to solve the issue. Fortunately, the Administration Manager was an excellent manager or the staff would never have been so good natured. I arranged for there to be a joint meeting between Administration and Marketing to try to resolve this conflict, with me facilitating.

I asked each of the bosses to *explain what had been going on* (step one). This was just a general conversation-opener mainly for me and them to diagnose what was happening and to display what the approach of each party would be to each other. They both spoke in business language. My interpretation was to listen to what they were saying and to follow, at the same time, the People Procedure. Administration explained their time constraint, that they needed three days to process an order and were given 24 hours. Marketing explained that they did not always get a warning themselves about when a brochure was to go out.

10   *People Models and People Procedure*

(At this point, in practice, I would be registering which People Model was seen as the most useful. In this instance, I chose the Myers Briggs Type Indicator (2009), which is discussed in Chapter 3.)

For now, I wondered if we would get a resolution because the Marketing Manager, by saying what he did, was stalling. I drilled down into the Marketing Manager. I was trying to establish an equal solution. "When *exactly* did you get such little notice?" Fortunately, he answered truthfully. "Not all the time. Just sometimes." "How often *exactly* is sometimes?" He didn't remember. "How long does it take, sometimes?" "Four days to one day." "Why does it take sometimes four days?" "Why does it take sometimes one day?" He doesn't answer the questions but says: "It shouldn't take less than three days." He also admitted that Marketing could push back on those who were responsible for giving him the go-ahead on the brochures. This 'meant' that he accepted the Administration's claim. I was half way to getting a commitment to an equal solution.

The next stage is to dive into the underlying needs of the two parties. Not to establish 'causes'. I am not interested in the latter partly because they often constitute the excuses and partly because people go on and on describing them. What can you do about causes if they are historical? You forget them and move on. With the Administration Manager and the Marketing Manager, I focused them on their personal needs. For the former it was to not work on weekends and for the latter it was to have an easy life. He didn't want all these complaints, tension and arguments with Administration.

The next stage is to discern the dominant theme of the discussion. This contrasts with figuring out the impact each party has on the other. The dominant theme in this example was that the Administration people and their needs were looked over; passed over. For me, being overlooked was a much larger systemic issue that I dealt with as a consultant over many years.

Commentary 1.1 summarizes the questions and interventions I actually made and took under the People Procedure. A standard problem-solving approach/ Business Procedure is set out on the left hand side. The latter is hypothetical as, obviously, I followed the People Procedure side of the table.

The People Procedure is as much diagnostic as action based. That way it will dig deep. It engages also in the personal aspects to the conflict (wanting an easy life is relevant in the previous example).

The six different People Models

The six different People Models I use in the book are outlined briefly below. One model I use to understand and work with organizational conflict, in Chapter 2, is a Partner–Ally–Friend model. An Ally assumes that other organizations are there to join forces with to fight a common enemy. A Partner is there to create an alliance with, add to a network, enlarge distribution channels. A Friend is in it for the long term; this is a sustainable trusting relationship. Different organizations have different assumptions about what the nature of a relationship is and should be. In this chapter, we unravel several organizations who merged or acquired another and explore the

Commentary 1.1 The People Procedure applied to Administration and Marketing

Business Procedure	People Procedure
What has been **going** on?	What has been **going** on? *This is a diagnostic question about the situation between the two people.*
What are their respective **positions**? *Admin: Not getting three days' notice; Marketing: can't commit to three days, it is out of our hands.*	What does the **People Model** say? *One of the six People Models would be used here. Using the MBTI on this example is explained in Chapter 3.*
Do you want a **proportionate** solution (based on power, resources, size etc.)? *At first, Marketing wanted more control and 'say' (because of their position in the organization). A Business Procedure would likely have left Marketing as king pin.*	Do they want an **equal** solution (each party being treated equally)? *In the end, after intervention by me, Marketing implicitly agreed to an 'equal' approach. This occurred when he admitted he could push back on those who were responsible for giving the go-ahead to him on the brochures.*
What are the **causes** of these issues? *The causes are historical and dictated by the rest of the organization. 'It just happens like that'.*	What are the **underlying needs** of the two parties? *The underlying needs were to prevent working on the weekend (Admin) and to have an easy life without all these complaints (Marketing).*
What is the **impact** of A on B and vice versa? *Impact on Marketing is little except for the inevitable complaints. Impact on Admin people was great. The business didn't suffer much because of the good nature of Admin. Coordination is the dominant business theme.*	What is the **dominant theme** of the whole discussion? *Admin being looked over, ignored in the first place, was the dominant theme.*
What are the **potential solutions**? *Potential solutions really look like Marketing will largely 'win'.*	Do the parties **want** to get to a solution? *After the parties had established a relationship, yes they both wanted to get to a solution.*
What is the **best possible** solution? *Marketing commits to giving as much notice as they can but doesn't promise anything.*	What is the **resolution**? *Marketing commits to giving three days' notice to Admin. They can do this by managing backwards, which they knew they could do. They established a friendship and Admin and Marketing got together with me for a two day workshop to work through all the relevant issues on the boundary of the two teams.*

12 *People Models and People Procedure*

M&As from the perspective of this People Model. Several mini case studies are used to illustrate: Sir Alex Ferguson, Angela Merkel and Richard Branson.

The second model used in the book, in Chapter 3, is the Myers Briggs Type Indicator (MBTI) (2009). (Later, I use the models of Carl Jung.) The MBTI describes four dimensions which explain how we relate to the world and how we take in and process information. There are several anecdotes which help to illustrate the consequences of the MBTI for conflict in different groups of people. Theresa May is the case study for the MBTI.

The third model I use in the book (in Chapter 4) is from Will Schutz (1984). I have used his framework in my earlier books (Garden, 2000, 2015, 2017). In this approach there are three dimensions, each reflecting different basic needs. These are: Inclusion (the need to exist, interact with others, stamp one's individuality on the world); Control is about the need for control, to establish competency and perform; Openness (or Affection) describes the nature of relationships (warm or cold, short term or long term). The model is illustrated by the case study of Sir Alex Ferguson.

Fourth is the Gestalt world of experience (in Chapter 5). The primary aspect of this is the Cycle of Experience. The main stages of this are: Awareness, Mobilization, Action, Contact, Resolution (see Nevis, 2001). The key issue I deal with here is whether or not a stage is 'interrupted'. We look at several examples of interpersonal conflict where this did happen as well as examples of different defence mechanisms. The case study at the end is of Flight Centre (FCTG) and their Family, Village, Tribe approach (Johnson, 2005).

The fifth model, in Chapter 6, is Jung's model of inner conflict. This pertains to the relationship between the individual and their world. We use several anecdotes to illustrate various examples of development of functions and individuation. Richard Branson is the case study.

The sixth People Model, in Chapter 7, is called the Life Conflicts Model. It is crafted from three of the frameworks I use and admire that tell you how to live a life. The first source of inspiration is Frankl's search for meaning (Existence). The second is John Haidt's Elevation and the third is Bandura's Self-Efficacy (or Efficacy). The case study is of Steve Jobs.

These are the six models used in the book to describe reality and to explain how, why and what conflict emerges. You can use all six models or stay with one or two preferred models. They serve as a different lens to view an organization. They pinpoint the meaning of the conflict and why it exists. They each apply at the inter-organizational, organization, Divisional, team, interpersonal, individual as well as inner level.

In the Applications chapter, Chapter 8, the People Models are applied. We look at several politicians: Barack Obama, Hillary Clinton, Donald Trump and Tony Blair through the eyes of the People Models.

Table 1.5 sets out the contributions of the six models.

(Dugan (2015, pp. 113–119) similarly uses a 'nested' theory of conflict.)

A summary of the book is in Table 1.6. Note that assigning a level to each chapter is solely for the purposes of creating enough order in the book and in the ideas.

People Models and People Procedure 13

Table 1.5 Differing contributions of the six models

Partner–Ally–Friend	• Use between two or more organizations or any other level • Looks specifically at relationships • Examines the roles involved • Constructive
Myers Briggs Type Indicator	• Pinpoints pre-existing conflict • Can analyse the individual, organization and any other level • Non-judgemental • Has in-built criteria to resolve conflict
Inclusion–Control–Openness	• Looks at underlying needs • Can focus on social–psychological interaction • Can look at inner conflict • Can be related to any level in the organization
Gestalt	• Focuses on general flow of experience • Describes conflict as arising from general behavioural patterns • Can use at individual, organizational level and any other • Focuses on energy and awareness
Carl Jung	• Can use at individual, organizational or any level • Widens potential of individual or organization • Explains seemingly irrational dynamics • Expands psychic space
Life conflicts	• Can use at any level • Looks at how to live a life • Constructive • Conflict arises when not fulfilling the People Model

Table 1.6 Summary of the book

Chapter	People Model	Level
Chapter 1	Procedure for conflict resolution	Overview
Chapter 2	Partner–Ally–Friend	Conflict between organizations
Chapter 3	Myers Briggs Type Indicator (MBTI)	Conflict within organizations (structure)
Chapter 4	Inclusion–Control–Openness (Will Schutz)	Conflict within organizations (team)
Chapter 5	Gestalt	Interpersonal conflict
Chapter 6	Carl Jung	Inner conflict
Chapter 7	Life Conflicts	Individual
Chapter 8	Applications	Primarily individual

Values

The context for the book is my own set of values. Listed below are the ones I am conscious of holding.

1 Most people regard conflict as a waste of time and unnecessary. However, it is not always destructive. Most theoreticians and researchers would allow

14 *People Models and People Procedure*

for it to be positive; that it can be functional rather than dysfunctional. In the many workshops I have run for managers I frequently put them in a game or simulation. I got used to monitoring the amount of conflict generated within each team. It was a near-certainty that if the group got stuck half-way through and went back to square one to figure out the solution, with commensurate loud voices and arguments, they were more likely to crack the answer and do a good exercise. The conflict was functional and led mostly to higher performance. Of course, this phenomenon was evident also in work in the organization. There is something about the capacity to go back to the drawing board which is associated with positive conflict. It can stretch you. It may be necessary for creativity.

2   Conflict is emotionally based so we need to deal with the emotional side of it not shut it down or cut it off. This is in contrast to authors who advocate putting 'the people' to one side during negotiations. In this book, the emphasis is squarely on people, even if they are emotional.

3   We need an honourable decent solution for both parties not just a solution that fits best interests. In the Introduction, I referred to two anecdotes, in both of which there was an equal solution, or at least an equal process. In the case of the bully Finance Director in the Introduction, during my intervention he had no special rights over his direct report. They were both treated equally; as equal human beings. Without this premise, or value, you will not get to a real or workable solution.

4   Each People Model leads to enlargement of psychic space. There is always a route to development in each model. Sometimes that might mean your own development, sometimes someone else's and sometimes the whole organization or part of it.

5   Workable conflict is when you can resolve it. Unworkable conflict is when you can't completely resolve it, need to learn to live with it and develop a modus operandi to work around it. Sometimes you go for the latter.

Conclusion

In this chapter, we have opened our horizons to incorporate people-language not just business-language. This involved getting a snapshot of the six different People Models used in the book as tools to help you resolve conflict. You can treat them like a pick and mix and adopt 'favourites'. That might mean you read and apply only a few of the chapters.

In each chapter, there is a set of exercises/questions and a checklist about the People Model. Be flexible and creative with these.

Exercises

1   What, to you, are the angels and demons involved in conflict? Do the angels win?

2 Can you describe your organization in MBA language and in People language? Write a few short sentences about it using each language.
3 Why should all organizations be treated as if they are equal? What will happen if they are/are not?
4 Why should all people be treated as if they are equal? What will happen if they are/are not?
5 Describe the (i) causes of an organizational intervention and then (ii) set out their underlying needs. What is the advantage of doing the latter and not the former?
6 What is the most important step, to you, in the People Procedure? Why?
7 What do you think you are really doing when you figure out the dominant theme? Why is this related to the People Procedure and not the Business Procedure?
8 What, to you, looks like the most interesting People Model?
9 What would be the easiest People Model for you to use?
10 What are the most important values in dealing with conflict?

References

Deutch, M. (2015). A brief history of social psychological theorising about conflict. In Woodhouse, T., Miall, H., Ramsbotham, D. and Mitchell, C. eds. *The contemporary conflict resolution reader.* Cambridge, UK. Polity Press.

Dugan, M. (2015). A nested theory of conflict. In Woodhouse, T., Miall, H., Ramsbotham, D. and Mitchell, C. eds. *The contemporary conflict resolution reader.* Cambridge, UK. Polity Press.

Garden, A. (2000). *Reading the mind of the organization.* Aldershot, UK. Gower Publishing Limited.

Garden, A. (2015). *Roles of organization development.* Aldershot, UK. Gower Publishing Limited.

Garden, A. (2017). *Organizational change in practice.* Oxford, UK. Routledge.

Johnson, M. (2005). Family, Village, Tribe: the evolution of Flight Centre. Sydney, Australia. William Heinemann.

Morrill, C. and Rudes, D. S. (2010). Conflict resolution in organizations. *Annual Review of Law and Social Sciences,* 6, 627–651.

Myers, I. B., McCaulley, M. H., Quenk, N. L., Hammer, A. C. (2009). *MBTI manual,* 3rd edition. Mountain View, CA. CPP Inc.

Nevis, E. (2001). *Organizational consulting: a gestalt approach.* Cambridge, MA. Gestalt Press.

Pinker, S. (2015). The better angels of our nature: why violence has declined. In Woodhouse, T., Miall, H., Ramsbotham, D. and Mitchell, C. eds. *The contemporary conflict resolution reader.* Cambridge, UK. Polity Press.

Schellenberg, J. A. (1996). *Conflict resolution: theory, research, and practice.* Albany, NY. State University of New York Press.

Schutz, W. (1984). *The truth option.* Berkeley, CA. Ten Speed Press.

2 Relationships between organizations

The computer users' groups

I was once hired by three autonomous but conflicted computer users' groups in Europe. One was relatively small and the other two moderate sized, one larger than the other. There were many arguments among them especially concerning the idea of having one large organization representing all of them, with the three separate organizations merged into one. The main justification for this was that it would leave them all more powerful and more dominant in the computer market. If they weren't 'strong' enough, didn't have enough 'weapons', it wouldn't help to 'win the war'. To an outsider, the questions arose "what war?", "what weapons?" but that was how these computer groups saw the world. (This is a logic suggesting the user groups were all 'Allies' – a term I use to describe a particular kind of nature or relationship type especially as it relates to organizations involved in mergers and acquisitions (M&As) or alliances. This chapter is oriented to exploring this concept.)

In order to test out whether these three groups should merge, I, at the request of some of the leading lights of the three organizations, held a workshop with all groups represented. The workshop was for two days with about 16/17 people, many of whom were loud and boisterous. To succeed in this workshop required me to be the most bossy and aggressive I have ever been and I had to deal head on with constant conflict. I ran them, initially, separated into three groups corresponding to their computer user groups. Everyone had to speak. By the end of Day One, it was evident that all three groups could accommodate the concept of 'one organization'. The final resolution agreed at the end of Day One, then, was to merge all three together although there was still conflict concerning how this would come about. Day Two was spent on implementation. Here the three groups were mixed, with conflict and arguments still occurring but less so. I let them coast much of the day steering them with discussion points. By the end of the second day, it was deemed a highly successful workshop and the powers that be were pleased with the outcome.

What did it add that I knew they were all Allies? One factor was that I had some idea of how they would behave and could be prepared for it. First, I knew they would try, early on, to beat me in an argument and that I had to win it.

Second, I gave them very clear tasks, goals and guidelines. I knew to stick to time and so on. This was not so much to express the Allies' nature but partly to control it. I knew not to expect them to be very creative but to steamroller through the workshop. They wanted to 'win'. As it turned out, 'winning' meant agreeing to a merger and 'losing' would have happened if they didn't agree to a merger. Structuring the workshop half way through with people from mixed computer user groups was equivalent to putting them 'on the same side'. It worked. It was very interesting to have all three of the user groups an Ally. Later on in the chapter, we will look at integration where the parties are mixed.

Dealing with conflict like this is, as I have indicated in Chapter 1, part and parcel of what I do as a consultant. In this chapter, we explore one particular angle of this subject of conflict; that is, of relationships *between* organizations. The People Model I use, the Partner–Ally–Friend model, can be used at any level; individuals, teams or organizations.

Key points in this chapter

Key points in this chapter are set out in Table 2.1.

M&As: business language

One primary relationship *between* organizations is that of mergers, acquisitions and alliances. How an organization manages any conflict has an impact on the success of that integration.

Most analyses, research and theory in this area are business-focused. In other words, it is MBA-speak, not PhD-speak. In general, motivations for M&As are drawn from finance and economic theory. The business logic focuses on "achieving a larger asset base, entering new markets, generating greater market shares/ additional manufacturing capacities and gaining complementary strengths and

Table 2.1 Key points in this chapter

- Merging the computer groups
- Key points in this chapter
- M&A and alliances: business language and theories
- An acquisition that is on tenterhooks
- Some research on knowledge-based workers
- The People Procedure
- People Model: Partner–Ally–Friend
- Conflict between the two
- Conflict in the voluntary sector
- Getting to yes: how it relates to this People Model
- Four organizations merged into one: the case of the public sector
- Conclusion
- Case studies: Sir Alex Ferguson, Angela Merkel, Richard Branson
- Exercises
- Checklists

18 *Relationships between organizations*

competencies, to become more competitive in the market place" (Gupta, 2012, p. 60). Where are the human factors? They come afterwards when people are attempting to explain why the M&A didn't work.

Initially, there was little attention in the academic literature on human factors. When it did arise, it was expressed as interest in culture. Even then, Marks and Mirvis (2011) state that

> we know that culture matters in merger and acquisition success. However ... we have seen that managing culture usually receives low priority by executives who are overwhelmed by the operational aspects of integration ... most of these same executives acknowledge that underestimating the importance and difficulty of combining cultures was a major oversight in their integration efforts.
>
> (p. 651)

The People Models described in this book are a far cry from just a cultural analysis. They look at People from all sorts of angles (see Weber and Schweiger, 1992).

An acquisition that is on tenterhooks

I was once hired to teach the managers of a company which had just bought out a small, very successful electronics company, which I shall call X. The message I had to give them was that they, in the acquiring company were, for the most part, to 'not go near the new company'. Specifically, they were trying to not over-manage them and decided that that meant the great majority of managers and staff would not interact closely with them.

The primary reason they wanted this was that there was an enormous danger of mismanagement and conflict because X was small and they were large. They needed a massive cultural shift to do it internally and they had never achieved that before. They did not need 'one culture' but two cultures. The whole point of what they were doing was to leave the small organization's culture alone, to cultivate it. X was creative and the acquiring company wanted to keep it that way.

I told the managers about some research I had done at London Business School about small rapid growth software companies in Cambridge Science Park, UK, and what makes the employees tick. One lesson from this research was the idea that there was a small organization type of manager and a large organization type of manager. What I had seen in the small (0–50 people), medium (150–250 people) and large sized companies (1500 people) was that when the company reached medium size they started looking round for a 'good' manager (in accordance with the received wisdom from venture capitalists and banks). However, a manager who is good in a large organization is lousy once installed in the small or medium sized organization. The problem in a nutshell was always conflict from over-control; over-management. My client, the larger acquiring company, trying to accommodate company X, was in the middle of this lesson. They chose the management team (who were known to be good people managers) who would be the point of contact with X. They were picked very carefully.

Research backs up the acquiring company's approach

In the research study I did at London Business School, I was primarily interested in the differences between job excitement, job motivation and job satisfaction as they emerged in the small software companies. Did job excitement lessen in larger sized companies? Yes. But job satisfaction got higher. Managers who talk of keeping knowledge workers satisfied rather than keeping them alert and on-the-go are a great concern.

These employees wanted to feel job excitement even in the largest organization. The managers there didn't know how to talk about it. This was the source of ongoing conflict.

Factors associated with job excitement

Different organizational factors were associated with each state. The satisfaction factors were resources, salary and perks, things the company can give to the employee. They have an overall sense of the employee being provided for, given to, looked after.

The factors associated with job motivation were simple: interesting work and career advancement.

The conditions that were associated with job excitement were the individual feeling useful, being fully used, being aware of making a contribution to the success of the company and doing challenging work. These relate to feeling stretched and with feeling that their inner resources, talents and skills are being used. These variables involve a sense of wanting to contribute to the company rather than wanting the company to contribute to them. To give rather than be given to.

Taking over a small, successful, creative organization like X is harder than it looks if you focus simply on the business factors involved. It is more subtle than that; the potential sources of conflict are rooted in what makes the employees of the acquired company tick.

Another way to get to grips with this way of viewing the world is the People Procedure, to which we now turn.

The People Procedure applied to the acquisition

Step one of the People Procedure: background and context

The acquiring company, used to being a large, action-oriented company, needed hearts and minds to be retrained for this new acquisition to be a success. Action-man managers that they were, they needed to sit still and wonder for a while

20   *Relationships between organizations*

before doing anything to the new company. The point was that these managers had to think and act more psychologically and wisely than they were used to. It was growing-up time.

The People Model: Partner–Ally–Friend

Step two of the People Procedure: the People Model – Partner–Ally–Friend

One People Model that can be used to help this process is explained below. My focus is on the *relationship* between integrating organizations and the assumptions about the nature of the relationship that exists between them.

There are three different kinds of relationships: Partner, Ally and Friend.

The *Partner* focuses on alliances between two or more organizations. This is the relationship type of company X, the acquired company. Here the term 'alliance' does not equate with a strategic alliance but simply as you would use the term with human beings; like a companion. Partners like to exist in a quasi-network with other organizations having collegial relationships. Fundamentally, they believe every organization is equal and aren't overly convinced of hierarchical relationships except to get tasks done. They rely on nimbleness. They can be a bit distant in relationships. Losing a Partner is not a disaster; they just pick up another one.

When a Partner has an alliance with another organization the other organization may be an Ally or Friend. It might or might not work well. It will if the organizations are good at managing relationships and not just the business.

- Collegial
- Not overly convinced of hierarchy
- Rely on nimbleness in individuals and organizations
- Like networks of individuals and organizations
- Like to be objective and independent

The *Ally*, in contrast, focuses on winning. This is the relationship type of the acquiring company. They are very competitive and like to be top-dog even with their merged or acquired or allied organization. They like to get the other organization to side with them, join forces with them to beat the enemy (the competition). They tend to be cut-throat with the latter and want the other organization to be so too. If they are not, the Ally will be confused and frustrated. The reason the Ally joins forces with another organization at all is to give them a greater chance of winning. They are a bit cut-and-dried, want events to keep moving fast and are action-oriented (sometimes to a fault).

- Winning is all
- Competitive
- Like to be top dog
- Action-oriented (sometimes to a fault)
- Can be cut-throat in behaviour

A *Friend* relates to another organization in order to have a stable friend whom they can do business with. They are looking for a long-lasting relationship and want to cultivate trust. The way to kill a Friend's good humour is to do something untrustworthy or disloyal even where there are good business reasons to do the latter. To a Friend, the relationship will be worthwhile if they continue to develop the friendship through different business ventures. They do not understand the idea of joining forces to beat an enemy (Ally), or picking and choosing other organizations as alliances (Partner).

- Trust is all
- Want relationships to be enduring
- Invest in the relationship
- Never be disloyal around one
- Long lasting as a general principle is valued

These are the relationship models that are present in integrating organizations. When an organization has assumptions about the nature of the relationship that differ from the other's, all sorts of conflicts can ensue.

Conflicts between the two

Partner and Ally. The Partner's primary motivation is flexibility in the market place. The Ally's isn't: it is winning in the market place. The Partner likes quite a broad reach but the Ally isn't necessarily interested in breadth but focus. Partners will be polite to the Ally but the Ally doesn't necessarily need that. They want the Partner to get straight down to business rather than engage in small chat. Partners tend to have more meetings than Allies would like. Allies won't always understand the sensitivities of Partners and vice versa. Table 2.2 illustrates.

Partner and Friend. A Partner is like quicksilver and the Friend wants longevity. The Partner wants breadth and the Friend wants depth (they want to trust their Partner). The crossed wires here come from the fact that the Partner is quite comfortable with superficial relationships and the Friend is left floundering with them. They want deeper connections. Table 2.3 illustrates.

Friend and Ally. This combination is probably the hardest to get right. The Ally is a strong position in business terms but the Friend is a strong position

Table 2.2 Partners and Allies

Partner's effect on Ally	Ally's effect on Partner
• Polite	• Get straight down to business
• Talk a lot	• Act
• Want breadth	• Want focus

22 *Relationships between organizations*

Table 2.3 Partners and Friends

Partner's effect on Friend	Friend's effect on Partner
• Quicksilver	• Longevity
• Breadth	• Depth
• Work alongside each other	• Work with each other

in relationship terms. An Ally will try to walk all over a Friend but behind the scenes the Friend will be trying to create the relationship it wants. One is medium term (Ally) and the other is long term (Friend). These assumptions could, if integrated, be a powerful relationship but they will only be so if the two organizations respect each other. Table 2.4 illustrates.

In the situation with the acquisition, we have a Partner and an Ally. The latter's propensity to act was matched by the Partner's nimbleness, apart from their tendency to talk a lot. The Partner was convivial and, more important, intent on retaining their *flexibility*. Their assumption was that everyone was a colleague. The acquiring company, an Ally, wanted to 'win' with their acquisition. They were still hard-driving and results-focused.

Step three of the People Procedure: proportionate or equal

The third stage of the People Procedure is to make sure organizations and people are treated equally (PhD speak) rather than proportionate to the organization's size, money, resources, power (MBA speak). The logic of an equal solution is that different units need equal air time. They need to be treated as equal to their status as one human being. All units have a modus operandi, a way of doing things that are legitimate. Therefore, they need to be treated equally. One of my most important interventions as a consultant is to establish that this equality exists.

In the case of the acquisition with X, what mattered was that their attitude of being in learning mode towards the acquired company enabled them to adapt more to the smaller organization. The latter knew more than they did about running an entrepreneurial company, about managing talent, about keeping talent in-house, about creating job excitement and so on. This was some way towards an equal solution.

Table 2.4 Friends and Allies

Friend's effect on Ally	Ally's effect on Friend
• Strong on relationship	• Strong on business
• Will try to create right relationship	• Will try to walk all over Friend
• Long term	• Medium term

Relationships between organizations 23

Step four of the People Procedure: underlying needs and feelings

Company X's underlying need was to be left alone as much as was possible and reasonable. My client's underlying need was to integrate the acquisition properly because everyone was watching them.

Step five of the People Procedure: dominant theme

The dominant theme was *consideration* by both parties.

Step six of the People Procedure: did they want a solution?

Both wanted a solution to the relationship issues (actual and potential) and were prepared to listen to advice.

Step seven of the People Procedure: resolution

The resolution was (a) to be open, (b) to be in learning mode, (c) to not assume anyone knew anything about acquisitions and (d) to constantly monitor the process.

Conflict in the voluntary sector

The worst cases of conflict in organizations, for me, have been in the voluntary sector. In one instance, it was in the psychological/educational arena. For quite a few years, people in the UK interested in the Myers Briggs Type Indicator (MBTI) met and communicated as the 'Myers Briggs Users' Group'. As numbers grew and the professionalization of the MBTI also proceeded, pressure came on us to re-invent ourselves as the British Association of Psychological Type, BAPT (to match the US Association of Psychological Type, APT). Some of us, mostly me, had had contact with the American crew. This was partly in relation to being formally trained in the MBTI to teach their APT Qualifying programme but also to do with my research using the MBTI and speaking at an APT conference.

We started BAPT with the election of officers – with me ending as President and the rest of the formal BAPT leadership positions being filled with MBTI fanatics (like me) who had been using the instrument for years. At the same time, another organization was being formed, the Oxford Psychologists Press (OPP), an independent distributor of psychological instruments. I was, initially at least, on the board of OPP.

BAPT was a Friend, APT was a Partner and OPP an Ally. The conflict between the three was gargantuan. First and foremost the conflict arose because neither APT nor OPP had an assumption that all three organizations were 'equal' (see the People Procedure in Chapter 1). They used power and

24 *Relationships between organizations*

size to get their own way. We in BAPT fumed. We thought our messianic fervour would be enough to justify being treated as equals. At OPP I was betrayed at one point at which time I left the Board (to a Friend betrayal is a disaster). At one point, OPP made the allegation to APT that I was a 'friend' of the Marketing Director – the idea that being a friend was wrong was music to the ears of an Ally but very strange to a Friend. In any case we weren't friends but more acquaintances – a subtlety that would mean everything to a Friend but not so much to an Ally. APT, as a Partner, wanted someone to do business with and OPP had the business model they wanted. So they chose OPP to liaise with and not BAPT. Why not both organizations? It was a mystery to us. APT was threatened by the longevity and expertise in the BAPT group, our preoccupation with Carl Jung and the fact that we had a mind of our own. Our strength was in monitoring and encouraging the ethical use of type not just the effective use of type.

The dominant theme was conflict and more conflict. Neither APT nor OPP were interested in working through this as they had their business needs met.

The resolution was that BAPT grew up and became a stand-alone organization with its own activities. I eventually resigned from all my posts.

Negotiating to Yes

Perhaps the most popular approach that deals with conflict is Fisher and Ury's Getting to Yes (2015). They presented their model as a third way to negotiate. While it is not exactly the same idea as companies merging and acquiring, the similarities in the two models are nevertheless close.

The first two ways of negotiating in Fisher and Ury's model are the two we typically use the most and, according to their model, shouldn't. The first way is soft bargaining where the negotiator "wants to avoid personal conflict and so makes concessions readily to reach agreement. He or she wants an amicable resolution" (p. 244). Notice that this way, termed 'soft', describes the modus operandi of a Friend in my model but the latter is not dysfunctional but highly functional.

SOFT
- Participants are friends
- Trust others
- Try to avoid a contest of wills
- **[FRIENDS]**

The hard negotiator sees any "situation as a contest of wills in which the side that takes the more extreme positions and holds out longer fares better. He or she wants to win" (p. 244). The 'hard' negotiator corresponds with the Ally who wants to win. Again, this strategy is simply another modus operandi that is equally real and functional.

HARD
- Participants are adversaries
- Distrust others
- Want to win
- **[ALLY]**

The third way is neither hard nor soft. It corresponds, in my model, with the Partner. For Fisher and Ury this is the method of principled negotiation. This method is to decide issues on their merits rather than through a haggling process focused on what each side says it will and won't do. It suggests that you look for mutual gains whenever possible and that, where your interests conflict, you should insist that the result be based on some fair standards independent of the will of the other side (p. 244). This slight standing back and independence is the equivalent of the Partner.

PRINCIPLED
- Participants are problem solvers
- Independent of trust
- Develop multiple options
- **[PARTNER]**

Note that, while there is only one 'right way' with Fischer and Ury, all three relationship types in my model are acceptable.

Four organizations merge into one: the case of the public sector

In the following anecdote, I explore a merged organization which was predominantly a Partner with pockets of Ally and Friend.

Step one of the People Procedure: background and context

I once acted as a Government Principal Advisor inside a public sector organization that consisted of four separate organizations merging and then merged into one. They each had their own position in the public sector but the common element was that they were all 'business-facing' – a trait that did not bode well for operating with People Model assumptions rather than business model assumptions (as per Chapter 1). (Note that I shift levels in the following and use this People Model as it can potentially be used: to describe the different merged organizations, the organization as a whole, sub-parts of the organization, individuals and so on.) A lot of time was spent by everyone in the organization, including the CEO and the deputy CEs, as well as the consultants all over the organization, in figuring out how to make this large organization work. Pretty quickly, the four organizations became eight Divisions. One was hived off as a separate organization in order to better meet its

26 *Relationships between organizations*

statutory requirements and we were left with seven Divisions (out of the four organizations). The speed at the beginning was rapid and pretty soon we had the obligatory Town Hall meetings. These were good. However, it all became mostly illusory pretty fast. Once the 'takeover specialists' had finished their contracts, the senior leaders were left largely on their own. They floundered with the People stuff. One would have to suspect that they had been chosen for no other reason than their prowess at MBA/business language. Conflict was rife in the organization for two reasons. One was the emotional conflict that is engendered by a merger, period: the feeling of annihilation felt by some of the groups/people. Second, people didn't agree with how the merger was being dealt with.

For example, I was involved, one year in, in participating in interviews of the eight members of the senior team, individually, for the purposes of holding an engagement survey. The interviews were led by an external engagement provider. None of the senior leaders spoke people/PhD language; it was 90–95 per cent business/MBA language. The problem is we were talking about engagement. I was totally bewildered. At the end of the survey, we tried to get the senior team to commit to engagement action steps they could take. But they couldn't do it. They talked themselves through two meetings and came up with nothing. Why? They would have been talking a foreign language. They simply could not figure it out and couldn't agree to any actions as a team.

One of the reasons for this state of affairs was that the senior team relied on the Communications Division to manage the people stuff. They were convinced that the senior team should be 'selling' to the troops and, as a result, each of the senior team members would produce broadsheets for their Division talking all the time about the wins of the last few weeks or months. Managing the people side of a merger is light years away from 'selling' manoeuvres orchestrated by the Communications Division. The 'wins' were primarily business-focused anyway. They had all missed the point.

Step two of the People Procedure: the People Model

The senior management team were largely Partners, including the CEO. The most powerful Deputy was an Ally. However, the merged organization as a whole was a Partner: they interacted a great deal with other organizations and people without steaming ahead to win (Ally) and without needing long-lasting friendships (Friend).

In the organization as a whole, consensus was the order of the day (Partner). The CEO had run his previous organization like this (a much smaller organization), including with a *collegial* way of practice and culture (Partner). This meant listening to all the different voices in the organization and making sure everyone else listened to others. They talked a lot but didn't get decisions or actions. Staff morale could have been better but they had no real way of making it so. They simply didn't have those skills.

Relationships between organizations 27

Step three of the People Procedure: proportionate or equal

The assumption of the CEO was that everyone should be treated equally. This was not, in my view, the attitude of his deputies. This would, then, be an issue for the organization as a whole.

Step four of the People Procedure: underlying needs and feelings

The next step of the People Procedure is to determine the underlying needs of the organizations. The merged organization, as a Partner, has the underlying needs shown in Table 2.5.

However, hidden in the organization are pockets of Ally – the relationship type of one of the previously merged organizations – and pockets of Friend – from the smallest-merged original organization. These pockets, if you heard them, were aware one year in that they were slowly being annihilated (their 'way' was). The most visible sign of this was that senior and middle managers from those pockets were being made redundant at a rapid pace, or being fired. Note that the Partner's way is not to build (Friend), it is to change Partners. The Allies, for their part, were seen as too aggressive and forceful. The Partner group at the top carried on regardless not really aware that such a dynamic existed in the organization. They weren't aware they were getting rid of two of the previously merged organizations because they couldn't 'hear' people language.

Step five of the People Procedure: dominant theme

The top team could not get anything done in the organization as the top team. They managed their own fiefdoms quite actively and in accordance with whether they were Partner, Ally or Friend. However, the dominant cultural preference was still the Partner. Overriding the issue of what their relationship type was, was the frustration that they could not get things done particularly as it related to people issues.

Table 2.5 Underlying needs of relationship types

Partner	Ally	Friend
• Flexibility	• Winning	• Building
• Breadth/coverage	• Height (being first)	• Depth
• Interest	• Smarts	• Friendships
• Speed	• Strength	• Common sense
• Cover more bases	• Fight the market place	• Win more customers
• Interacts widely	• Plans well	• Shares resources
• Disengages easily	• Protective	• Can stay silent
• Easily adds more organizations	• Wants to be a hero and action man	• Builds on existing relationships
• Effectiveness	• Efficacy	• Ethical
• Don't go to work, go to play	• Go to work to work hard	• Go to work because they love it

28 *Relationships between organizations*

Step six of the People Procedure: did they want a solution?

The participants did, in fact, seem to want a solution to the fact that they talked so much instead of taking action, so this step in the People Procedure was not an issue.

Step seven of the People Procedure: resolution

There wasn't one. For example, the senior team and some middle managers toyed with doing a cultural analysis as a way of getting to grips with the people side but stalled over it, discussing it up, down and sideways. I had left before they made a decision about it.

Conclusion

In this chapter we have looked at two organizations in the private sector, a voluntary sector one and a public sector merger. The differences in organizational rationale, structure of the organization and processes are as different as can be. But the people processes have been exactly the same. The dynamic of conflict I found was similar irrespective of the business factors and the apparent cause of it. In the remaining chapters I stick to the same formula: business organizations are mixed with public sector organizations and analysed with People Models.

Relationships between organizations   29

Case studies: Sir Alex Ferguson, Angela Merkel, Richard Branson

In this section on case studies, we look at the relationship type of well-known figures – Sir Alex Ferguson, Angela Merkel and Richard Branson. While these are individuals and not organizations, it is easier to drill down to the former to demonstrate the principle of the People Model.

Sir Alex Ferguson

My first case study demonstrates the Friend, as opposed to the Ally or Partner. It is an extract of a book by Sir Alex Ferguson, the legendary manager of Manchester United Football Club for 23 years and winner of an unprecedented number of trophies. I chose him because he is such a character, as well as being an interesting exemplar of the Friend. (He serves also as my case study in Chapter 4.) In the letter he is writing to Eric Cantona, a famous and superb player working under Sir Alex, there is looming a parting of the ways and potential conflict and Cantona has not been turning up for training.

> [the important thing for me is] to remind you how good a player you were for Manchester United and how grateful I am for the service you gave me. I will never forget that and I hope you won't either.
>
> You are always welcome here and if you just pop in unexpectedly for a cup of tea, no fanfare, just for a chat as friends, that would mean more to me than anything. Eric you know where I am if you need me and now that you are no longer one of my players, I hope you know you have a friend.
>
> (The Archives, Ferguson, 2015)

Not much chance of conflict there with a mature Friend approach.

Angela Merkel

Angela Merkel is primarily an Ally as is illustrated in the following excerpts from Kornelius (2013, pp. 54–56).

> she is extremely pragmatic when there is a chance of reaching a compromise … she always wants a result.… A new characteristic emerged: the pleasure of competition, the excitement of victory … She admitted to a liking for the cut and thrust of political argument and seeing through the tactics used by opponents … "I told him that the time would come when I would get him in a corner too … the day will come. I'm looking forward to it".… Merkel began to revel in competition: kill or be killed. Be better than the others in order to deprive them of the advantage.… "Its rather like sinking a battleship – I feel great whenever I score a hit".

30 *Relationships between organizations*

Richard Branson

Richard Branson is an entrepreneur, and in this passage focuses on his business Virgin Unite. This business is not just another charity, but would become an integral part of Virgin Group philosophy. It is run mostly on the lines of the Partner model:

> in our newly connected world … it's not about throwing charity at issues – it's about working in partnership with people on the frontlines to turn those issues into opportunities.… I'm talking about the power of the ordinary, everyday person to become entrepreneurs and change-makers to set up their own businesses, to seek their own fortune and be in control of their own lives.
>
> (Branson, 2011, pp. 4–6)

Exercises

The following section gives you some exercises with which to practise the Partner–Ally–Friend model.

1. Determine whether your organization is a Partner, Ally or Friend. What are the key attributes or actions that make you give this description or assessment?
2. Now determine an example of two organizations, which are of the other relationship types. What are the key attributes or actions that make you give this description or assessment?
3. Describe any M&A or alliance between your organization and any other organization. Describe the process in MBA language.
4. Now describe it in PhD language (Partners, Allies, Friends).
5. Why, to you, does the spirit of excitement get less the larger the organization?
6. Describe the ways in which Fischer and Ury's model of resolving conflict is different from the Partner–Ally–Friend model.
7. What are the main sources of conflict for a Partner?
8. What are the main sources of conflict for an Ally?
9. What are the main sources of conflict for a Friend?
10. Do you think, as I do, that treating the other party as an equal, ignoring size, profit, assets, is the most fundamental principle to achieve in a merger, acquisition or alliance?

Checklist 2.1 Assessing Partner–Ally–Friend

Mark each question from 1 (low) to 7 (high). You can assess organizations, parts of an organization, teams and individuals.

Then tally the scores up.

Partner	Items	Mark 1–7
1	Collegial	1(low).........2.........3.........4.........5.........6..........7(high)
2	Likes breadth	1(low).........2.........3.........4.........5.........6..........7(high)
3	Likes many alliances/deals	1(low).........2.........3.........4.........5.........6..........7(high)
4	Independent	1(low).........2.........3.........4.........5.........6..........7(high)
5	Objective	1(low).........2.........3.........4.........5.........6..........7(high)
6	Can be superficial in relationships	1(low).........2.........3.........4.........5.........6..........7(high)
7	Talks a lot	1(low).........2.........3.........4.........5.........6..........7(high)

Partner total =

Ally	Items	Mark 1–7
1	Likes to win	1(low).........2.........3.........4.........5.........6..........7(high)
2	Forceful	1(low).........2.........3.........4.........5.........6..........7(high)
3	Likes 'weapons' to use for the organization	1(low).........2.........3.........4.........5.........6..........7(high)
4	Always has a 'game plan'	1(low).........2.........3.........4.........5.........6..........7(high)
5	A bit insensitive	1(low).........2.........3.........4.........5.........6..........7(high)
6	Courage	1(low).........2.........3.........4.........5.........6..........7(high)
7	Action-oriented	1(low).........2.........3.........4.........5.........6..........7(high)

Ally total =

Copyright material from Annamaria Garden (2018), *How to Resolve Conflict in Organizations*, Routledge

Friend	Item	Mark 1–7
1	Believes in long-lasting relationships	1(low)........2.........3.........4.........5.........6.........7(high)
2	Trust is key	1(low)........2.........3.........4.........5.........6.........7(high)
3	Friendly	1(low)........2.........3.........4.........5.........6.........7(high)
4	Likes depth	1(low)........2.........3.........4.........5.........6.........7(high)
5	Prefers wisdom to cleverness	1(low)........2.........3.........4.........5.........6.........7(high)
6	Attracts customers	1(low)........2.........3.........4.........5.........6.........7(high)
7	Likes to build up	1(low)........2.........3.........4.........5.........6.........7(high)

Friend total =

Relationship type	Total score

Partner

Ally

Friend

Copyright material from Annamaria Garden (2018), *How to Resolve Conflict in Organizations*, Routledge

References

Branson, R. (2011). *Screw business as usual*. London, UK. Virgin Books.

Ferguson, A. (2015). *Leading*. London, UK. Hodder & Stoughton.

Fisher, R. and Ury, W. (2015). Getting to yes: negotiating agreement without giving in. In Woodhouse, T., Miall, H., Ramsbotham, D. and Mitchell, C. eds. *The contemporary conflict resolution reader*. Cambridge, UK. Polity Press.

Gupta, P. D. (2012). Mergers and acquisitions (M&A): the strategic concepts for the nuptials of corporate sector. *Innovative Journal of Business and Management*, 1, 60–68.

Kornelius, S. (2013). *Angela Merkel*. Richmond, UK. Alma Books.

Marks, M. L. and Mirvis, P. H. (2011). A framework for the human resources role in managing conflict in mergers and acquisitions. *Human Resource Management*, 50, 5, pp. 651–670.

Weber, Y. and Schweiger, D. A. (1992). Top management cultural conflict in mergers and acquisitions: a lesson from anthropology. *International Journal of Conflict Management*, 3, pp. 1–17.

3 Conflict within organizations – structure

A classic framework

There is a great deal of theory and research on organizational effectiveness. There is much less on conflict in organizations. Within the latter there is a lot of research on teams (which will be explored in the next chapter) or interpersonal contexts (Chapter 5). However, there is one framework, a classic one by Pondy (1967), which looks at what I call 'structural conflict'. In this chapter, I make use of this approach as well as one People Model I know well, the Myers Briggs Type Indicator (MBTI) (Myers *et al.*, 2009).

Pondy's framework looks at the organization more than the individual. Most of my consulting work is for the organization as a whole. Even work I am hired to do for an individual is done within the context of what is going on in the organization and what change processes are under way. The framework consists of a breakdown of conflict into three areas: functional or lateral, bureaucratic, and bargaining. Each of these relates to some aspect of the structure of the organization. As far as functional or lateral conflict is concerned, "Analysis of the problems of coordination is the especial province of this model" (Pondy, 1967, p. 298). The essence of the bureaucratic model is "the need to control by the boss and the drive for autonomy by the direct report" (p. 314). The focus of bargaining warfare is the "competition for scarce resources ... [one of the aspects of this is] the battle between staff and line" (p. 297). We explore all three in what follows.

Key points in this chapter

Table 3.1 sets out the key points in this chapter.

Functional or lateral conflict

"Goal divergence is the source of conflict when two parties who must cooperate on some joint activity are unable to reach a consensus on concerted action" (Pondy, 1967, p. 300). Organizational arrangements are frequently designed to prevent this happening, e.g. plans, schedules and job descriptions, which define and delimit subunit responsibilities.

Table 3.1 Key points in this chapter

- Pondy's functional, bureaucratic and bargaining conflict
- Key points in this chapter
- Functional or lateral conflict
- The Administration and Marketing Departments
- People Model: the MBTI
- Cautions around using the MBTI
- Bureaucratic conflict
- The retail company
- Bargaining conflict
- Annihilating HR
- Conclusion
- Case study: Theresa May
- Exercises
- Checklists

In lateral conflict, no one person has more direct hierarchical power, by definition. What happens? The parties concerned can have a bias. Or, you can have an equal solution, i.e. an honourable solution. It depends on the sophistication of the parties at developing a relationship. Sometimes you need an adjudicator.

The Administration and Marketing departments

In our first example of structural conflict, the adjudicator was me. In Chapter 1, I described an example to illustrate the People Procedure. It explored the conflict arising between two Administration and Marketing Managers because the former was given last minute work to do mailing out the company's brochures when they needed three days' notice. I orchestrated a meeting between the two parties to resolve it. However, when outlining the People Procedure in Chapter 1, we didn't have a People Model to illustrate the relationships involved. Now we do. In this chapter I explore the same anecdote using the Myers Briggs Type Indicator (MBTI).

Both Managers had done the MBTI with me in another context. The Administration Manager was typed an 'ISTP' (Introverted, Sensing, Thinking, Perceiving) and the Marketing Manager an 'ENFP' (Extraverted, Intuitive, Feeling, Perceiving). In what follows, I will explain what those labels mean, and also whether we should use labels at all.

The People Model: the MBTI

I chose the MBTI to use in this organization partly because I had used it extensively there and in other organizations. Aside from that, it is one of the most widely used personality measures in the world. It is a gauge of people's cognitive style and classifies people into 16 different psychological types. It claims to be an operationalization of Jung's theory of types (which it may not be strictly;

36 *Conflict within organizations – structure*

see Garden, 1991). It was created by Isobel Myers around the time of the Second World War with help and inspiration from her mother Katherine Briggs. It is popular for good reason: it is *non-judgemental*. The MBTI is a model to identify individual preferences that are of equal value. It is useful in highlighting some simple differences between people which can lead to conflict or variations in style, career preference, time horizon, style in managing projects and so on. Pinpointing these and the implications for any change in behaviour required was one of my aims. It is important to note, however, that a difference in personality type per se does not necessarily lead to conflict. Quite the contrary. It can lead to accommodating alternative ways of doing things, integration, synergy, symbiosis, etc.

You do not, however, need to actually use the questionnaire to discover which type you are. You can use reflection and observation instead.

There are four dichotomous dimensions in the MBTI. People tend to prefer one aspect of each pair more than the other. For the most part, for example, they choose Extraversion more than Introversion or Introversion more than Extraversion.

1   *Extraversion (E) and Introversion (I).* These two opposites relate to how you orient yourself to people and take in energy. In the extraverted attitude "energy and attention flow out, or are drawn out, to the objects and people in the environment. The individual experiences a desire to act on the environment, to affirm its importance, to increase its effect" (Myers *et al.*, 2009, p. 26). In the Introverted attitude,

> energy is drawn from the environment toward inner experience and reflection. One desires to ... affirm [the] value [of the internal state]. The main interests of the Introverted type are in the world of concepts, ideas [feelings] and inner experiences.
>
> (p. 26)

2   *Sensing (S) and Intuition (N).* These two opposites relate to how you take in information. Sensing refers to the (five) senses. Sensing establishes what exists. "Persons oriented toward Sensing focus on their immediate experiences available to their five senses. They, therefore, often develop characteristics ... such as enjoyment of the present moment, realism ... practicality" (p. 24). Intuition "refers to perception of possibilities, meanings and ... insight ... including possible future events. People who prefer Intuition may develop the characteristics that can follow from that emphasis and become imaginative, theoretical, abstract, future oriented and original or creative" (p. 24).

3   *Thinking (T) and Feeling (F).* These two opposites relate to how you make decisions. Thinking is the function that comes to a decision by linking ideas together through logical connections. Thinking relies on principles of cause and effect. "Persons who are primarily oriented toward Thinking are likely

Conflict within organizations – structure   37

to develop ... analytical inclination, objectivity, concern with principles of justice and fairness, criticality" (p. 24). Feeling is the function by which

> one comes to decisions by weighing relative values and merits of the issues.... They try to understand people and to anticipate and take into account the effects of the decision at hand on the people involved and on what is important to them.
>
> (pp. 24–25)

4   *Judging (J) and Perceiving (P).* These two opposites relate to how you deal with your outer world. In the Judging attitude, a person is concerned with

> making decisions, seeking closure, planning operations, or organizing activities ... in the Judging attitude, perception tends to shut off as soon as they have observed enough to make a decision. In contrast, people who prefer the Perceiving attitude will often suspend judgement to take another look.... Persons who characteristically live in the Perceiving attitude seem in their outer behaviour to be spontaneous, curious, adaptable, and open to what is new and changeable.
>
> (p. 25)

Thus, you end up on one side or the other of each of the four dimensions. None is superior to any other. There are no 'right' or 'wrong' answers. Choices between the paired opposites are forced, creating 16 psychological types. Table 3.2 illustrates the basic descriptors.

The dominant function

(The next section is complex. You can skip it if you want to.) One further refinement of the basic theory I have outlined is that one of the two middle functions is the 'dominant', or primary, and the other is called the 'auxiliary', or secondary function. The basic rule for determining the dominant is this: for *an Extravert* (like the Marketing Manager), if you are a perceiving type then Sensing or Intuition is dominant. If you are a Judging type then Thinking or Feeling is your dominant. The Marketing Manager is an Extraverted Intuitive Feeling Perceiving type. Since he is an Extravert and a Perceiving type, then Intuition is his dominant. If you are

Table 3.2 Basic descriptors of the MBTI dimensions

Extraversion	• Talking, outer, active, breadth
Introversion	• Reflection, inner, independent, depth
Sensing	• Detail, practical, accurate, careful
Intuition	• Overview, conceptual, imagination, symbolic
Thinking	• Logic, cut-and-dried, analytical, objective
Feeling	• Values, considerate, appreciative, people-oriented
Judging	• Order, timelines, sequential, measured, steady
Perceiving	• Adventurous, spontaneous, last-minute, risk-taker

38   *Conflict within organizations – structure*

an Introvert like the Administration Manager, and a Perceiving type, the formula is quite different. If you are a Perceiving type your dominant is Thinking or Feeling. If you are a Judging type your dominant is Sensing or Intuitive. In other words, the dominant of the Administration Manager was Thinking.

Pinpointing the conflict between Administration and Marketing

The MBTI provides us with a hint of potential sources of conflict, first, for the Administration and Marketing departments and, second, for the two Managers tasked with solving the conflict. The profile for the departments is in Table 3.3. The dominant type for the Administration department is ISFJ (Introvert, Sensing, Feeling, Judging). For the Marketing department it is ENFP (Extravert, Intuition, Feeling, Perceiving).

This is what we can conclude from the MBTI of the departments. Note that three of the four dimensions are different.

1   The Administration department is likely to keep more to themselves than Marketing. The two don't have strong relationships even though their work overlapped.
2   Administration focuses on accuracy and detail (Sensing) and Marketing focuses on the big picture (Intuition).
3   Both are Feeling so there should be grounds for sympathy for each other's position.
4   The Judging function in Administration holds the key to the main issue. Judging types appreciate clear and firm timelines, boundaries, order, being measured and steady. These would all be disrupted by having Marketing give

Table 3.3 The MBTI of the Administration and Marketing departments

Administration		Marketing	
E..×...............I		E..........×...I	
Extravert	Introvert	Extravert	Introvert
S..........×...N		S...×.........N	
Sensing	Intuitive	Sensing	Intuitive
T...×.........F		T..×...................F	
Thinking	Feeling	Thinking	Feeling
J..........×...P		J...×..............P	
Judging	Perceiving	Judging	Perceiving

them short notice to do the brochures. On the other hand, with a Perceiving attitude, Marketing people will prefer to fly by the seat of their pants and do things at the last minute. This is the fundamental conflict on the ground.

This breakdown clarifies the context for the two departments. If we look at the MBTI of the two Managers, we get an idea of how the 'negotiation' between them will go. Table 3.4 sets out the MBTI profile for the Administration Manager and the Marketing Manager.

Remember that the Administration Manager had preferences for Introversion, Sensing, Thinking and Perceiving (ISTP) and the Marketing Manager had preferences for Extraverted, Intuitive, Feeling and Perceiving, (ENFP). Here again, three of the four dimensions are different. However, that does not mean they are in conflict.

I might assume that Sensing and Intuition are highly relevant to this conflict; the difference is stark. However, I ignored it. This is because they communicated very easily in terms of Sensing language and Intuitive language. I ignored also the Thinking and Feeling difference. The Administration Manager, while being a Thinking type, was such a skilled people manager, especially at dealing with Feeling, that I ignored this difference too. These were not implicated in this conflict.

However, we are still left with two dimensions, Extraversion and Introversion which is key to the conflict and Judging and Perceiving which is key to the resolution of the conflict.

The dominant theme of this relationship was that Administration was being looked over. This was partly because Introversion takes more time than Extraversion and needs to think things through (see Myers *et al.*, 2009, p. 336). Clearly, the Introversion in the Administration Manager had waited while this

Table 3.4 The MBTI of the Administration and Marketing Managers

Administration Manager		*Marketing Manager*	
E...................................×.................I		E.........×.................................I	
Extravert	Introvert	Extravert	Introvert
S..........×..........................x..........N		S.................................×..........N	
Sensing	Intuitive	Sensing	Intuitive
T...................×.......................F		T...............................×.............F	
Thinking	Feeling	Thinking	Feeling
J.................................×..........P		J..................................×.........P	
Judging	Perceiving	Judging	Perceiving

40 *Conflict within organizations – structure*

situation carried on. Introversion is unwilling to dominate the environment and will put off tackling conflict. An Extravert would be likely to have acted sooner. At a deeper level, Introversion is 'looked over' by Extraversion. This is what has happened. They put up with things by adapting inside rather than creating an adaptation outside.

In the organization as a whole, it was true that Administration was looked down on. My interpretation was that this was partly because they were nice! and partly because their educational level was lower than Marketing (who mostly had degrees) and from Investment (who had degrees from Oxford and Cambridge and were the apparent kingpins of the lot). I reasoned, in my interventions, that it was the environmental context that was partly responsible for the current predicament and was forever trying to shore up Admin.

Notice that the bosses of these two (ISFJ – Introverted, Sensing, Feeling and Judging – and INFP – Introverted, Intuitive, Feeling and Perceiving) were each likely to tell these two managers to resolve the situation themselves. The latter are both at a similar level in the hierarchy. There is no one else to resolve it but the Administration Manager and the Marketing Manager.

The joint Perceiving attitude is the basis for resolution of the conflict. The way they got to a resolution was by establishing an honourable modus operandi and by creating a relationship. Neither of them was very structured. Both did things on the spot. They made decisions on the spot if they had a previous context. And so they did. Both focused on play and that was the pattern of their interaction. They talked as their non-work selves, horsing around. They did develop an actual relationship which continued outside the meeting. These were the components of the resolution. That they did resolve the conflict was referred to in Chapter 1. The agreement was that Marketing would give three days' notice to Admin, which is what the situation required.

Cautions around using the MBTI

When I used to go to APT (Association of Psychological Type) conferences I would be given a badge with my INFP (Introverted, Intuitive, Feeling, Perceiving) label on it. I wouldn't wear it. These are some cautions around using the MBTI. My primary one is around identifying too much with your type!

- Having a closed mind.
- Labelling yourself and others "You're an INFP" or "You're *not* an INFP!"
- Limiting yourself to only those aspects in the MBTI profile "I'm an INFP so I will be good with people."
- Limiting yourself to not doing those things associated with your opposite "I am an INFP so I won't be good at managing, thank you."
- Limiting others in exactly the same way as above. "You're an ISTJ; you'll be good at paperwork."

I have heard countless people break these cautions.

Bureaucratic conflict

Each form of structural conflict (functional, bureaucratic and bargaining) is rife in organizations but probably the one I am most used to dealing with as a consultant is the *bureaucratic* form, i.e. that between boss and direct report. The essence of this dynamic is the battle of wills over control between them. Pondy states that the

> bureaucratic model ... is appropriate for the analysis of conflicts along the vertical dimension of a hierarchy.... Vertical conflicts in an organization usually arise because superiors attempt to control the behavior of subordinates, and subordinates resist such control.... Control over the conditions of one's own existence ... is highly valued in organizations, particularly in large organizations. The subordinate, therefore, perceives himself to be threatened by and in conflict with his superiors, who are attempting to decrease his autonomy.
>
> (1967, pp. 314–315)

In the anecdote that follows, I have explained a case where the MBTI was used deliberately as a catalyst for very necessary change in a company and to avoid unnecessary conflict. The lessons for using the MBTI are different from our previous example, the Administration and Marketing Managers.

The retail company

Step one of the People Procedure: background and context

The conflict was potentially extreme in this next example. My client was a retail company spread throughout the UK. At the time I was called into action, this company had been bought out by a consortium of senior managers from other companies and retail experts. They constituted the most senior management level in the company. Since the retail company was not doing very well, was challenged with its own survival, they had a raft of ideas and policies they believed would rescue this woebegone company. My task, as consultant, was to transform the rest of the organization – starting with their direct reports, the Regional Managers (RMs) – to align it with this new broom in the senior managers in HQ.

The solution, supported by the senior managers, was a five-day workshop for all of the RMs. There was certainly work to do. I remember, for example, a conversation on every workshop we ran for the RMs, about whether or not they should be called 'Sir' or 'Mr' by staff. It was a very serious issue to them. They had always been called one of these two.

Their bosses, the senior managers, wanted to be called by their first names and wanted the RMs to be called the same. I, or my partner-consultant, would always trigger this conversation with the RMs at some stage. Whatever the outcome, we were always rescued by the planned visit of one of the Directors to

42 *Conflict within organizations – structure*

one of the meals on the workshops by having him state to the RMs that they must refer to him by his first name.

Step two of the People Procedure: what is the nature of the People Model: MBTI

The new senior managers tended to be savvy with People Models and could talk about them including the whole idea of empowerment. The MBTI had already been administered on a workshop for the senior managers and Directors. The RMs were unaware of the instrument before that time.

What does the profile of the RMs mean? In the case of the RMs, their MBTI profile for that group compared with the MBTI profile for the senior group spoke volumes. Table 3.5 illustrates.

Are there potential sources of conflict here?

a Extraversion (E) and Introversion (I)

No issues. This distribution was typical in a range of populations. It was typical, at the time, of UK managers in general.

b Sensing (S) and Intuition (N)

The first aspect that will play out with the SN dimension is that there are so many Sensing types among the RMs. What might this mean? Their preference is likely to be with structure, tradition, hierarchy, the present. They will pay little attention to the future, new things, novelty, abstract data, lateral working. However, the senior managers, with their preference for Intuition will expect the

Table 3.5 The MBTI profile of the RMs and their senior managers

Regional Managers		*Senior Managers*	
E.....................×..............................I		E............................×...............................I	
Extravert	Introvert	Extravert	Introvert
S.....×...N		S.......................................×.................N	
Sensing	Intuitive	Sensing	Intuitive
T..×...F		T.....×..F	
Thinking	Feeling	Thinking	Feeling
J........ ×...P		J...×.................P	
Judging	Perceiving	Judging	Perceiving

latter in the behaviour of the RMs. With the MBTI, we were able to make explicit these personality differences. The Sensing-dominated RMs were expected to think more long term (not just to the end of the year) – adopt more modern procedures, and to not be so hierarchical with the store managers and their staff.

c Thinking (T) and Feeling(F)

This dimension is an issue because it is so strongly a preference for Thinking compared with Feeling for both the senior managers and RMs. It means a focus on thinking, logic, cause-and-effect rather than a focus on people, context, emotion. Any adaptation of this preference might well come from the expectations and demands of store managers and staff, however, not the senior managers.

d Judging and Perceiving

There is only a small minority of the RMs who have a Perceiving preference. The majority have a Judging preference. This difference with the senior managers is possibly the most likely to create conflict. The Judging preference wants order, time, priorities while the Perceiving type prefers excitement, adaptability, openness and time flexibility. The senior managers will want more of the latter from the RMs. They, on the other hand, may not see that this has any validity.

Step three of the People Procedure: proportionate or equal

In other words, do the senior managers have an honourable solution? Or, do they just order the RMs about? They had a mostly honourable solution; not perfect. In spite of their frustrations with the RMs they treated them with respect.

Step four of the People Procedure: underlying needs and feelings

Step four of the procedure examines the underlying needs in the relationship between the RMs and the senior managers. Whatever the behaviour, people in the situation will be trying to get underlying needs satisfied even if those needs are hidden from them. With the RMs, the underlying needs are allied to the MBTI and can be predicted from them. Table 3.6 illustrates.

Step five of the People Procedure: dominant theme

The next step in the procedure is to decipher the dominant theme of the interaction/relationship.

The dominant theme is *resistance to the challenge of the new*. There is a clash around the new. That is the main theme. The senior managers created terror in the RMs; they felt threatened, afraid for their jobs, negative, very critical and complaining. To the senior managers there was frustration, a sense of urgency,

44   *Conflict within organizations – structure*

Table 3.6 Underlying needs in the relationship

Regional Managers *Sensing Judging – SJ*	Senior Managers *Intuitive Perceiving – NP*
• Keep things the same	• Make everything new
• Old management style	• New management style
• The new senior managers should leave them alone	• Want more interaction with RMs and store managers
• Stability	• Flexibility
• 'Sir' or 'Mr'	• 'Bob' or 'Mark'
• They know what they are doing (as RMs)	• The RMs don't know everything after all
• Look to history	• Look to the future
• Seniority counts	• Expertise counts
• They know more about running stores than the new senior managers	• The senior managers know more about how other companies operate
• Want to be taken seriously	• Want to be taken seriously
• To be treated with respect	• To be treated with respect
• To have each new step examined thoroughly	• To transform the stores quickly to get moving to change now
• To have pride in the stores	• To have pride in the company

they were slowed down, negativity. The RMs' negative reactions were explored on the series of five day workshops. They moaned for at least the first day. Our limit was lunchtime on Day Two and then they had to stop and play ball with us. Their negativity was shifted to the positive from then on.

The essence of the conflict is located in the management of the stores and how that is carried out; with what management style?

Step six of the People Procedure: did they want a solution?

Both parties wanted a solution. The RMs recognized that they were dealing with a new context: the potential of losing their jobs. They wanted to know, from us, how to change.

Step seven of the People Procedure: resolution of the conflict

Being aware of the MBTI was helpful to all of them. It was useful to interpret it in a development way not just a descriptive way. At one level the MBTI taught them to (i) tolerate their opposite type. At another level it encouraged them to (ii) develop their opposite type. In this sense there were practical things that could be done to assist with this development. When using the MBTI as it should be used, the idea is to add non-preferred functions. At a third level we have a (iii) compromise between the two main MBTI groups (SJ types and NP types).

They need each other. You need SJ as well as NP for positive reasons. Together they complement each other. Finally, (iv) the stance of the senior managers was to not fire the RMs and hire new ones. They appreciated the depth of expertise in the company and went down the route of building the existing RMs instead. This was a major step to resolution of the conflict.

In this case, I have taken two of the four MBTI dimensions as open to potential conflict. My judgement on this stemmed partly from the fact that I was involved with the managers close up and could see the interactions with the senior managers as they occurred. However, there are no hard and fast rules that tell you when conflict is likely. Sometimes it is obvious and sometimes it is not.

In the next case we explore a situation where the MBTI appears to have no potential for conflict at all.

Bargaining conflict

The third aspect of structural conflict is called 'bargaining conflict' by Pondy (1967). This is designed to deal with conflict among interest groups in competition for scarce resources. This bargaining model is particularly appropriate for "the analysis of labour–management relations, budgeting processes and *staff-line conflicts*" (Pondy, 1967, p. 278, my emphasis). In this case I describe what happened in a battle between the staff and line.

Annihilating HR

For four years of my life I made the mistake of not being a consultant but being an employee. What made it worse was that, for the first time in my life, I was associated with HR. I was trained in Organizational Behaviour not HR and the two are entirely different. Nevertheless, I thought it would be all right as HR was 'to do with people'. A few years after joining I was involved in a change process, which I have described at some length in Organizational Change in Practice (2017). My focus was on the execrable incompetence of the large consulting company who ran the change process, designed to decimate HR. One year prior to that had been another change process also designed to decimate HR. Prior to that we had been a separate organization and, just as the merger was announced, there had been a review of, guess who: HR, designed to shrink it.

I wrote about my resistance to the latest change process in my 'change' book. My resistances went something like this:

- Passivity
- Meekness
- Zero positive intention
- Negativity
- Arguing to myself
- Rebellion
- Outspoken in certain places

46 *Conflict within organizations – structure*

- Avoidance of change team
- Staying out longer for lunch
- Went for numerous coffee catch ups
- Not working proper hours
- Sitting at desk for months doodling
- Throwing away papers
- Not cooperating with the handover team
- The longer it went on the worse I became.

(Garden, 2017, pp. 106–107)

Step one of the People Procedure: background and context

HR managers have maintained for a long time that the HR function is important for organizational effectiveness. They specify the key functions, and these are things the organization cannot apparently do without. In fact,

> most annual reports boldly state that the firm's people are its most important asset. However, despite these widely-held beliefs and all-too-frequent-statements, many organizational decisions suggest a relatively low priority on both the human resources of the firm and the Human Resources (HR) department.

(Barney and Wright, 1997, p. 3)

So it was with my employer who, belatedly, was intent on 'upskilling' or at least upgrading the organization's HR function and introducing strategic business partners.

Step two of the People Procedure: the People Model (the MBTI)

The MBTI profile of the HR function was known to me as I had administered it to each person there. There were 60 people and the MBTI profile was as in Table 3.7.

In other words, the different MBTI dimensions were roughly equal in terms of number of people. Some of the HR people described it as being 'balanced' which would have been a good thing. However, it wasn't. Given the new requirements being placed on HR it shouldn't have been as desirable to have equal numbers of the attitudes and functions. There was likely to be conflict between the HR numbers and the *context*.

Table 3.7 Numbers of type out of 60 possible

Extraverts	32	Introverts	28
Sensing	30	Intuition	30
Thinking	31	Feeling	29
Judging	27	Perceiving	33

The HR function was in a change process to (i) create strategic business partners who would function at a level which would be above the current top HR roles, and (ii) to increase the skill-use of the rest of HR so they were doing higher value work.

All of these things suggest a requirement for Intuition relative to Sensing; Intuition is more future-oriented and more strategic. It is also more developmental. Therefore, we should have seen more Intuitive representation than a Sensing–Intuition equality.

As far as the Thinking–Feeling dimension is concerned, we should have seen Feeling elevated over Thinking as there was an expectation for HR to do higher value work with people and less systems work.

Therefore, the MBTI profile was not the ideal one it was spoken of as being. In addition, the manager's MBTI was ISFJ (Introvert, Sensing, Feeling, Judging). He performed his role reasonably well but was disliked enormously by his boss for 'not performing'. What that meant none of us knew. The manager lived out his MBTI profile in a limiting and conflict-creating way: not doing various tasks because he "was an Introvert", for example. The stand-up meeting for that branch was cancelled by him when he first arrived and only put back after considerable time and pressure from others. His excuse was the MBTI. "Introversion" doesn't like that sort of thing. It doesn't matter if Introversion does not naturally gravitate to 'that sort of thing'. The MBTI approach should be: "Yes, I will do the stand-up and I will learn how to do it."

Step three of the People Procedure: proportionate or equal

The HR Branch Manager and the HR branch were barely consulted on the change process so I would have to say it was a power-based political solution not an equal honourable solution. The main protagonist of HR was, according to my reckoning, an ESTJ (Extravert, Sensing, Thinking, Judging). He used to accuse HR of being 'his overhead' and didn't want any HR people at all. He could justly be accused of wanting to annihilate HR. His bombastic superior style was what made many of HR traumatized by the whole process, even while we theoretically agreed with it.

Step four of the People Procedure: underlying needs and feelings

The underlying needs of the HR branch were to be left in their comfort zone. This included the manager. The underlying needs of the senior managers were to really shake HR up this time. The two sets of needs were mutually exclusive. The senior managers won. If the Branch had only woken themselves up by their own initiative the change process would not have been seen as necessary.

Step five of the People Procedure: dominant theme

The dominant theme was that the conflict was between *warring parties*, which wasn't necessary.

48 *Conflict within organizations – structure*

Step six of the People Procedure: did they want a solution?

The HR branch did not want this solution because they had no hand in creating it. The solution was created by a consulting company and the senior managers, both of whom did want *their* solution. However, because the HR did not want it, they stalled the implementation. I myself thought the idea of HR Business Partner a good one but loathed the incompetence of the change process and its gobbledygook and redundancy focus (Garden, 2017).

Step seven of the People Procedure: resolution

There was no resolution at the level of feelings. In practical reality, the 'resolution' was that the change process went ahead without the real cooperation of HR. In other words there was persistent conflict that went underground.

Moving on

As you might imagine, the HR staff who stayed (about 50 per cent) were conflicted about whether to stay or go, cooperate or fight. As were the Retail Managers in the example before that. Because of this, you need to insist that the use of the MBTI be constructive. It should never be used in selecting who to fire, for example. It should be positive, always.

Conclusion

In this chapter we have used the very popular MBTI to explore sources of conflict and how to resolve them. In spite of unresolved issues with the MBTI (Garden, 1991), it can still be used with care because its intent is to be constructive and developmental. Needless to say, the MBTI is often used with teams and individuals but it can also, as we have seen, be used at an organizational level.

The case study in this chapter is of Theresa May, the British Prime Minister at the time of writing, and immersed in conflict.

It is to teams we turn in the next chapter, albeit with a different People Model: Will Schutz's Inclusion–Control–Openness model.

Conflict within organizations – structure 49

Case study: Theresa May, British PM

Theresa May's MBTI, as deciphered using her biography (Cawthorne, 2016), is an Introverted, Sensing, Thinking/Feeling Judging person (IST/FJ). Remember that the following simply illustrates a *process* you can use. I have not asked her to do the MBTI; but that is the point. You can decipher it anyway.

Commentary 3.1 Theresa May and the MBTI

Theresa May's projected MBTI and quotes	*My commentary*
Introversion not Extraversion "she learnt self-reliance tinged with a certain shyness" (p. 4) "she was reticent and self-contained" (p. 7) "has no small talk whatsoever" (p. 41) "May was fundamentally unknowable, not given to small talk" (p. 89)	These quotes reflect classic Introversion but they are a bit jaundiced. Introversion is not inferior to Extraversion (see *Quiet* by Susan Cain, 2012). The benefits of introversion are authenticity, independence of thought, ability to be quiet and listen, an inner orientation to develop and so on.
Sensing not Intuition "I haven't built up too many expectations. I think it is better to actually get there and find out. I have to get there" (p. 23) "[as Home Secretary] she clung on by mastering her brief with what was said to be a microscopic attention to detail" (p. 40) 'she's such a details person" (p. 91) "she is more of a proficient corporate manager than a creative thinker or intellectual innovator" (p. 91)	Sensing has the advantage over Intuition in knowing and remembering detail and facts. All of this would be useful to a Prime Minister. It would also be beneficial, in that role, to develop some Intuition since it is a far-seeing role. Intuition also allows for more creativity.
Thinking more than Feeling? "in cold and icy terms she took him [Vince Cable] apart" (p. 40) "her tough-talking style" (p. 40) "The operational style … was a sort of bunker-ish mentality, that involved lots of briefing against other departments and Number Ten" (p. 40)	This dimension is the only one I am suspicious of. The data isn't persuasive enough to say they point to a Thinking type not a Feeling type. It is just possible she is the latter.
Judging not Perceiving "lacked spontaneity" (p. 5) "Her working style … is very closed, very controlling" (p. 88) "I respect her style – it is steady and serious. She is authoritative in parliament – superficial attacks on her bounce off" (p. 84)	The comments make clear her preference seems to be Judging. If she is rigid in this style she will immerse herself in conflict. The job is too big for a rigid Judging type, or a rigid Perceiving type. The positive Judging style is reflected in the data about her style being steady and serious.

50 *Conflict within organizations – structure*

Exercises

1 What are the key advantages of Extraversion and of Introversion? How might conflict between the two emerge?
2 What are the key advantages of Sensing and of Intuition? How might conflict between the two emerge?
3 What are the key advantages of Thinking and of Feeling? How might conflict between the two emerge?
4 What are the key advantages of Judging and of Perceiving? How might conflict between the two emerge?
5 Do you use your type as a label? Is this OK? Do you use the MBTI as a self-limiting excuse? How could you use type as a self-expanding thing?
6 Does your organization have any functional or lateral conflict? How would knowledge of the MBTI help you understand that conflict?
7 Does your organization have any bureaucratic conflict? How would a knowledge of the MBTI help you understand that conflict?
8 Does your organization have any bargaining conflict? How would knowledge of the MBTI help you understand that conflict?
9 How can you resolve conflict that has gone underground? Would knowledge of the MBTI help?
10 How does your organization as a whole need to develop in MBTI terms?

Checklist 3.1 The dynamic of type in the organization as a whole

Rate your organization on a scale from 1(low) to 7(high)

Extraversion–Introversion

Talking to everyone is a big thing (E)	1(low).........2.........3.........4.........5.........6.........7(high)
Prefer small group discussions (I)	1(low).........2.........3.........4.........5.........6.........7(high)
Prefer breadth (E)	1(low).........2.........3.........4.........5.........6.........7(high)
Prefer depth (I)	1(low).........2.........3.........4.........5.........6.........7(high)
Like to meet people (E)	1(low).........2.........3.........4.........5.........6.........7(high)
Like to get on with work (I)	1(low).........2.........3.........4.........5.........6.........7(high)
Noisy (E)	1(low).........2.........3.........4.........5.........6.........7(high)
Quiet (I)	1(low).........2.........3.........4.........5.........6.........7(high)
Total score out of 28 for each	Extraversion _____ Introversion _____

Sensing–Intuition

Overestimate time to complete things (S)	1(low).........2.........3.........4.........5.........6.........7(high)
Underestimate time to complete projects (N)	1(low).........2.........3.........4.........5.........6.........7(high)
Look to the past (S)	1(low).........2.........3.........4.........5.........6.........7(high)
Escape into the future (N)	1(low).........2.........3.........4.........5.........6.........7(high)
Can't imagine things (S)	1(low).........2.........3.........4.........5.........6.........7(high)
Not realistic (N)	1(low).........2.........3.........4.........5.........6.........7(high)
Too traditional (S)	1(low).........2.........3.........4.........5.........6.........7(high)
Ignore tradition too much (N)	1(low).........2.........3.........4.........5.........6.........7(high)
Total score out of 28 for each	Sensing _____ Intuition _____

Thinking–Feeling

Copyright material from Annamaria Garden (2018), *How to Resolve Conflict in Organizations*, Routledge

Too hard (T)	1(low)..........2..........3..........4..........5..........6..........7(high)
Too soft (F)	1(low)..........2..........3..........4..........5..........6..........7(high)
Too harsh decisions (T)	1(low)..........2..........3..........4..........5..........6..........7(high)
Gives in (F)	1(low)..........2..........3..........4..........5..........6..........7(high)
Competing (T)	1(low)..........2..........3..........4..........5..........6..........7(high)
Accommodating (F)	1(low)..........2..........3..........4..........5..........6..........7(high)
Needs to cooperate (T)	1(low)..........2..........3..........4..........5..........6..........7(high)
Needs to stand up for self (F)	1(low)..........2..........3..........4..........5..........6..........7(high)
Total score out of 28 each	Thinking _____ Feeling _____

Judging–Perceiving

Too pedestrian (J)	1(low)..........2..........3..........4..........5..........6..........7(high)
Too high risk (P)	1(low)..........2..........3..........4..........5..........6..........7(high)
Structures everything (J)	1(low)..........2..........3..........4..........5..........6..........7(high)
No structure (P)	1(low)..........2..........3..........4..........5..........6..........7(high)
Always planning ahead (J)	1(low)..........2..........3..........4..........5..........6..........7(high)
Seat of the pants (P)	1(low)..........2..........3..........4..........5..........6..........7(high)
Can't move them (J)	1(low)..........2..........3..........4..........5..........6..........7(high)
Too up and down (P)	1(low)..........2..........3..........4..........5..........6..........7(high)
Total score out of 28 each	Judging _____ Perceiving _____

Summary of organization
Place scores for the organization below:

Extraversion	Introversion
Sensing	Intuition
Thinking	Feeling
Judging	Perceiving

Where are the potential sources of conflict in this analysis?

Copyright material from Annamaria Garden (2018), *How to Resolve Conflict in Organizations*, Routledge

Checklist 3.2 Where do we need to develop as an organization?

In general, assess the development needs of the organization in terms of the MBTI.

Extraversion

Introversion

Sensing

Intuition

Thinking

Feeling

Judging

Perceiving

54 *Conflict within organizations – structure*

References

Barney, J. B. and Wright, P. M. (1997). On becoming a strategic partner: the role of human resources in gaining competitive advantage. *CAHRS Working paper series*. Cornell University ILR School.

Cain, S. (2012). *Quiet: the power of introverts in a world that can't stop talking*. New York, NY. Crown Publishing Group.

Cawthorne, N. (2016). *Theresa May: taking charge*. London, UK. Endeavour Press Ltd.

Garden, A. (1991). Unresolved issues with the MBTI. *Journal of Psychological Type*, 22, 3–14.

Garden, A. (2017). *Organizational change in practice*. Oxford, UK. Routledge.

Myers, I. B., McCaulley, M. H., Quenk, N. L., Hammer, A. C. (2009). *MBTI manual*, 3rd edn. Mountain View, CA. CPP Inc.

Pondy, L. R. (1967). Organizational conflict: concepts and models. *Administrative Science Quarterly*, 12, 2, 296–320.

4 Conflict within organizations – teams

The importance of teams

> Over the last forty years, teams have come to be considered as a central element in the functioning of organizations ... teams provide diversity in knowledge, attitudes, skills and experience, whose integration makes it possible to offer rapid, flexible and innovative responses to problems and challenges, promoting performance and improving the satisfaction of those making up the team.... However, teams do not always act in this way, and sometimes fail to achieve the high performance expected of them.... In fact, everyday experience tells us that in many cases teams, far from being mechanisms for capitalising effectively and satisfactorily on collective effort, turn into *black holes* that relentlessly consume the physical, mental and emotional energies of their members. This tends to involve their wasting a great deal of effort to attain their goals – if indeed those goals are met at all.
>
> (Rico *et al.*, 2011, p. 57; my emphasis)

In this chapter we explore conflict in teams. We explore one team which was the black hole Rico *et al.* talk about. Teams and team conflict are still a bit of a mystery. We are not really sure what makes them tick; what makes them work. Much research has been conducted to find out.

In general, researchers have recognized intragroup conflict as a core property that significantly influences group effectiveness (de Wit *et al.*, 2012). Thus, they have identified various features of group structure as antecedents of this type of conflict. A few studies have also raised the possibility that the psychological characteristics of group members matter. This is because such factors "can drive interpersonal dynamics in groups" (Varela *et al.*, 2008, p. 437).

The People Model I use in this chapter presumes that the latter claim is correct; that group members' psychological characteristics can drive interpersonal dynamics including conflict in groups. Table 4.1 sets out the key points in this chapter.

56 *Conflict within organizations – teams*

Key points in this chapter

Table 4.1 Key points in this chapter

- The importance of teams
- Key points in this chapter
- The Executive Committee who never met
- People Model (Will Schutz): Inclusion–Control–Openness
- Humming as a team
- Underlying needs
- Research on teams
- Digging deeper into the Inclusion–Control–Openness model
- The other Executive Committee
- Determining the main dimension
- Conclusion
- Case study: Sir Alex Ferguson
- Exercises
- Checklists

The Executive Committee who never met

Step one of the People Procedure: background and context

When I was working at London Business School, the Accountancy Professor suggested my name to a company in the City (of London) of which he was on the Board. I got the contract and started a fascinating journey with them, the first and most glaringly obvious piece of work to be done with the Executive Committee themselves as a team. They were a 'black hole'. They weren't even a group. They were six isolated individuals running their own fiefdoms with little recourse to each other even when making decisions that affected the whole Group. They never met as a team, had no strategy for the company or plans for it. Each individual empire was guarded jealously by the kingpin at the top. There was tremendous conflict between them that was all politely underground. My first two interventions were quite simply to create a team out of these disparate individuals. The Managing Director (MD) was relatively weak and focused on managing his own specialty, his own particular area. He didn't believe the company should have a strategy or plans, a view not shared by most of the rest of the Executive Committee. Backing into this thorny subject was a secondary priority of my first intervention.

They had hired a rather luxurious City-like venue for our first three days away. The tension was extreme. Within five minutes of opening, the MD announced that he thought the whole exercise was going to be a waste of time. I asked him how he would know whether it was a waste of time and promised him that if any of these signs became evident we would stop the team-building exercise and all go home. He outlined the signs he thought of and I put them on a flip chart. I checked with him if it was OK if we continue until we saw any of these signs that it was a waste of time. He agreed to carry on with this condition.

I had bamboozled him a little but, as long as I stayed completely calm, it seemed to work with him. We continued like that for three days making absolutely sure that what we were doing was not a waste of time. The team building exercise continued and, by the end of it, they had agreed to have weekly meetings as an Executive Committee and have lunch with each other occasionally. We had had some discussions, with no conclusions, about a strategy and needing to plan. We aired quite a few bases for conflict just by speaking openly. We had done the Myers Briggs Type Indicator, the Will Schutz measure and discussed these and various other exercises.

We knew also that the next layer of management should have a similar team building exercise. This 'lower' layer had complained in great detail (to me) about their defunct Executive Committee and wanted the whole company 'sorted' from top to bottom. At least the Executive Committee saw the need for such an exercise 'further down'.

This is an example that is rather stark. There was not enough agreement at an individual level to even have a team meeting. Similarly, there wasn't enough agreement to have a strategy or plans. However, after six months of these activities and after a second workshop focusing on a strategy and plans, the Executive Committee were unrecognizable. They had formed the bare bones of a team.

The People Model: Inclusion–Control–Openness

Step two of the People Procedure: the People Model – Inclusion–Control–Openness

The People Model I am going to use to clarify what was happening with this Executive Committee is drawn from the work of Will Schutz (1984). I have highlighted Will's work in each of my three books (Garden, 2000, 2015, 2017). His theory describes interpersonal behaviour in three dimensions. I have used this as extensively as the MBTI, for many years. I have always thought that it captured something very real about human beings. It is probably more confronting personally than the MBTI. Sometimes that is exactly what you need as a consultant. These same three dimensions explain the issues and sources of conflict faced by any team. These occur in a recognizable sequence.

The three phases of team development

The first phase is termed Inclusion. It is this that we have seen so far in the Executive Committee. The second dimension is called Control – which we shall see in the next phase of the team's development. The third phase is termed Openness, which the Executive Committee barely got to as they went round and round the Control issues for years (until the company was bought out and some of the Executive Committee were removed).

58　*Conflict within organizations – teams*

The Inclusion phase

The very first set of activities that occur or need to occur in the formation of a team, is to interact in a general way with the others present. This can take the form of generally sociable behaviours, introductions, discussion of who does what job and so on. These are termed 'Inclusion behaviours'. They continue until each member has 'introduced' themselves sufficiently and the vestiges of a team are thereby formed.

With the Executive Committee, a team was *initially* formed on our first three days away. Each of them had, one way or another, established themselves in the eyes of the others, claimed space and had a certain 'presence' vis-à-vis the others. This started to resolve, to some extent, the core issues of the Inclusion phase. Note that the basic underlying conflict in the Inclusion phase is between the individual and the group – between the individual's agenda and the group's: being unique and belonging to a group at the same time. Resolving this is what you are after.

The Control phase

The second phase of team formation is termed Control. During this phase, issues of authority, control, competitiveness, structure, means to an end and power are worked through. The basic conflict that needs to be resolved in this area is between spontaneity and control, in order for regeneration to occur. With the Executive Committee, this phase took the next five years and could have taken longer except that, as I have mentioned, the company was bought out and some of the senior people were removed.

They could not agree on anything relevant to this phase. The MD stopped any such resolution of the conflict in this area and the Finance Director also prevented resolution of many control issues for very different reasons. As indicated, the MD did not believe in strategy or plans because the government kept changing the rules for the industry; therefore, how could you plan anything? The others' response was that this was sticking your head in the sand and that they should, at least, do scenario planning. The basic conflict or issue was never really resolved.

Another key source of conflict in the Control area was talent. The Jugglers saw this as vital and wanted to develop the skills they had. The Bosses wanted to fire certain individuals and hire in new people.

The delegation of control further down the line was also never resolved. This was loosened then tightened then loosened then tightened. The next level down of managers learned to adapt to this Control behaviour but didn't like it and moaned to me incessantly about it. Much of the conflict here related to the degree of control each Committee member felt they should have particularly with respect to more junior staff. They found it very hard to delegate and truly empower. Some of the latter occurred. On the other hand, leadership was wanting and was hard to express with an MD who wasn't really acting as an MD.

Conflict within organizations – teams 59

The Openness phase

The Executive Committee never truly got to the point where they were dealing *fully* with the Openness and trust issues, the province of the Openness phase. As I have said, this is because they never got past circling round and round Control issues. The disadvantage is that a team only truly 'hums' when they move on to this final phase and face trust issues in the team. Since I cannot use my Executive Committee as an example, I will illustrate Openness issues with another team.

Humming as a team

A team that did truly 'hum' was a mix of six managers I worked with at IMD, the Swiss management school in Lausanne, Switzerland. I was their facilitator. They were on a two-week programme called Mobilising People. In the middle of the programme all teams spent three days up in the Swiss Alps. Day One was getting there. Day Two was spent abseiling and jumping off a bridge backwards. The evening of Day Two and Day Three was spent on a management game (see Chapter 5). After the bridge jumping was a boat race. My group didn't seem to have a hope. They were the lightest and slightest of all, individually. However, my group won. They did so because they were the most bonded and team-like of the six teams so they shot past everyone. The big brawny groups were whipped. My group had moved (superficially at least) from Inclusion through Control to Openness in just over a week; enough to make a difference.

General theory of the People Model

The general theory behind the People Model I have described can be applied to individuals, parts of organizations or organizations (see Garden, 2000). This is summarized in Table 4.2.

Table 4.2 General theory of Inclusion–Control–Openness

Inclusion	*Control*	*Openness*
• Interactions with others	• Control behaviour with others	• Trust with others and trustworthiness
• Introductions	• Authority	• Openness
• Boundaries with others	• Power and where it comes from	• Bonding with others and 'humming'
• The beginning of a process	• The execution of things	• Things coming to fruition
• Establishing your existence	• Talent and how to get it	• Rapport with others unlike you
• Identity	• Competence	• Likeability
• Being unique and in a group	• Spontaneity balancing control	• Giving to others first; not waiting

60 *Conflict within organizations – teams*

Step three of the People Procedure: proportionate or equal

Like true, polite City gents, the Executive Committee treated each other superficially as equal, with the exception of the MD who treated everyone else as inferior. While he listened to others when in their company, he basically took no notice of what anyone else said. The Executive Committee did, however, treat those more junior to them as 'not equal'; it was a very hierarchical company.

Step four of the People Procedure: underlying needs and feelings

The diagnosis so far for the Executive Committee has zeroed in on the Control dimension. However, until you reach the level of underlying needs in the situation it would be difficult to intervene successfully. Here, we are at the level of feelings that belong to each of the three dimensions Inclusion–Control–Openness. In general, the feelings associated with each are: Significance, Competence and Likeability respectively. Table 4.3 illustrates.

One of the factors illustrating that the people-state of the client organization stalled in the Control area was explained by the underlying needs in the company. There was masses of *resentment* that originated from the tendency to *blame* others and to hold others *responsible* for things they were not responsible for. It happened. I was blamed up, down and sideways for things that were nothing to do with me and seethed, having to act as if I didn't. This dynamic occurred from two sets of people; first the Executive Committee especially the Finance Director whom I was closely associated with. The people blamed by the Executive Committee resented this extremely. Second, the dynamic happened with the next level of senior managers (who reported into the Executive Committee). They constantly blamed the Finance Director for everything (and me by implication) and the latter (the Finance Director) felt enormous bitterness over this.

In sum, we had a seething pit of resentment and blaming (both control issues) throughout the organization, year on year.

Step five of the People Procedure: dominant theme

This was, in part, the dominant theme of the company. Very few people felt fully competent and successful there. There was no spontaneity. The blaming from the Executive Committee was one reason why, when I did initial interviews of managers, they said the Executive Committee were very hierarchical with them and that suited them fine – that way, they could get on with their jobs. On the other hand, the blaming by the next level down was worse than anything emanating from the Executive Committee.

Step six of the People Procedure: did they want a solution?

Yes, they did. They all experienced acute frustration without a solution. No one won without one.

Table 4.3 Underlying needs and feelings of the three dimensions

	Inclusion	*Control*	*Openness*
Underlying needs when this dimension is healthy and free of conflict	Significance, feel you belong, unique, feel you count, recognized, distinctive, you feel you exist, you notice and give recognition to others, feel special	Competence, everyone is responsible and no one is to blame, feel in control, people feel they have talent, admired, feel spontaneous	Likeability, people are aware of themselves and others, people feel liked, trusted, accepted, feel real, genuine, engaged, depth, commitment, purposeful
Underlying needs when there is a conflict or issue with this dimension	Feel excluded, invisible, ignored, valued only for doing a job not for yourself, feel invaded, talked over, interrupted, exhausted, feel that you don't count	Feel ridiculed, incompetent, resentment, chaotic, feel blamed, being made to feel responsible when you aren't, belittled, humiliated, stupid	Feel unappreciated, disliked, rejected, naive, suspicious, mistrusted, hatred, unaware of how others feel, hollow, empty, depressed, superficial, betrayed

62 *Conflict within organizations – teams*

Part seven of the People Procedure: resolution

The resolution of these conflicts involved a lot of time and energy from a range of people and, even then, was not full resolution. They involved the Executive Committee giving the senior managers more say in what happened in the company, especially for cross-organization activities. Once this had been done it required holding the Executive Committee to the fire while they went through a process of tolerating the way the senior managers did things. Mistakes needed to be worked through. The shift overall was towards a learning organization where (i) mistakes could be made and corrected, (ii) there was tolerance for doing things in different ways from the ways the Executive Committee members would do them. By the time I left there was still ample work to do to create a learning organization but they had made progress.

Table 4.4 sets out the core issue, or source of conflict, for the three dimensions.

Research on teams

Jehn and Mannix (2002) propose that conflict in work groups can be categorized into three types: "Relationship, task and process conflict. Relationship conflict, an awareness of interpersonal incompatibilities includes affective components such as feeling tensions and friction. Relationship conflict involved personal issues such as dislike among group members" (p. 238). In the Schutz model used in this chapter, relationship conflict would correspond with Openness, if anything. However, Schutz's definition is more extensive.

Task conflict, according to Jehn and Mannix, "is awareness of differences in views and opinions pertaining to a group task" (p. 238). This corresponds to a large extent with Schutz's Control dimension although the latter is more extensive. Jehn and Mannix create a third conflict dimension which they term 'process conflict'. It is defined as "an awareness of controversies about aspects of *how* task accomplishment will proceed" (p. 238, italics in the original). It "pertains to issues of duty and responsibility such as who should do what and how much responsibility different people should get" (p. 239). Note that this, once again, corresponds to the Control dimension in Schutz.

Chun and Choi (2014) do an interesting study and have their own definitions of conflict. They too have task conflict and relationship conflict but add 'status conflict' to reflect power needs. The latter is also equivalent to the Control dimension in Schutz's theory. So, Jehn and Mannix, as well as Chun and Choi, have two of their conflict dimensions relating to one Schutz dimension. They miss the Inclusion dimension completely.

Table 4.4 Core issues for each dimension

Inclusion	Control	Openness
Being unique and belonging to a group	Plan ahead and, at the same time, be spontaneous	Gives and trusts first without expectation

Conflict within organizations – teams 63

Digging deeper into the Inclusion–Control–Openness theory

The Inclusion–Control–Openness People Model describes different behaviours underlying which are specific core issues that need to be resolved. We have explored the path or process of this in teams across time. There is another dimension to this framework that comes from different *ways* of resolving the issues in each dimension.

Connoisseur or Populist

For example, there are different ways of resolving the Inclusion demands. I call these alternate ways, for simplification, the Connoisseur and the Populist. Table 4.5 describes. These are two extremes; people are just as likely to end up in the middle.

The Connoisseur resolves the Inclusion issues by interacting with a few people and focusing on quality not quantity. The Populist resolves the Inclusion issues by interacting with many people and focusing on quantity not quality. Neither way is better than the other. However, they may end up in conflict with each other. You can, of course, be a bit of both which can be a powerful position. When you do end up in the middle of this dimension you could, however, simply be confused.

In the company/case study in this chapter, the Executive Committee were, overall, Connoisseurs individually. However, they weren't very good at being Connoisseurs. They didn't work well at the Inclusion concerns.

The remaining managers in the company were for the most part Connoisseurs who, unlike their bosses, worked much harder at Inclusion concerns. They all prided themselves on having a product policy that rested on quality not quantity. The rest of the organization was, however, Populist; sociable, interacting. Figure 4.1 illustrates.

In other words, you can use this framework at two levels. The first is *whether* or how well a team or organization is resolving each of the core issues of the three dimensions. The second is in what *way* they are doing this. In the above instance the two alternatives are Connoisseur and Populist. The next section looks at the Juggler and Boss.

Juggler and Boss

There are also different ways of resolving the Control issues faced by any individual, team, Division, organization etc. I call these different ways, for

Table 4.5 Connoisseur and Populist

Connoisseur	*Populist*
• Own circle of friends	• Sociable
• Quality	• Quantity
• Like to work in small groups	• Like to work in large groups
• Low need for attention	• High need for attention

64 *Conflict within organizations – teams*

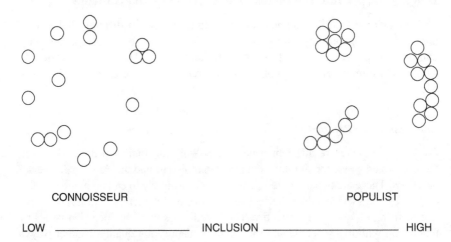

Figure 4.1 Connoisseur and Populist.

simplification, Juggler – which prefers low Control ways – and Boss – which prefers high Control ways. Being a combination of the two is a very powerful position or, otherwise, is a muddled confused state. Table 4.6 illustrates.

The Juggler prefers a focus on expertise and speed as a means to control what is going on and the achievement of results. The Boss prefers structure, power and authority, plans and systems to achieve the same results.

In the case we explored at the beginning of this chapter, the battleground was the Control dimension. This meant Juggler was in conflict with Boss. The Managing Director and two other Directors were Jugglers, to the wrath of the Finance Director and two others, who were Bosses. I have already mentioned that the MD did not believe in a strategy or plans for the company. This was because the government kept changing the rules for the industry; therefore, how could one plan anything? Instead, you should develop the company's ability for adapting to government (classic Juggler).

The Juggler tends to see as essential to build the talent you have got and the Boss tends to see this issue as firing people and hiring new talent. This conflict was resolved in practice in our example of this chapter by restraining the Bosses and using me to build the talent that was there. Figure 4.2 illustrates.

Table 4.6 Juggler and Boss

Juggler	Boss
• Controls through expertise	• Controls through power
• Agility; nimbleness	• Forearmed; plans
• Speed	• Size
• Resourcefulness	• Resources

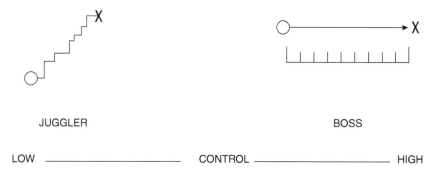

Figure 4.2 Juggler and Boss.

In one computer company I had a Juggler to deal with in the CEO/Chairman. His direct reports were mostly Boss. Many of the rest of the organization were Jugglers. The CEO struggled with the control-heavy style of his direct reports; who struggled with the low-Control style of their boss, the CEO. Whenever the latter spoke to the staff, however, there was a great connection; the boss being, at heart, a rebel. The CEO, through a series of workshops run by me and two other consultants, focused on loosening up the bureaucracy (i.e. too much Boss behaviour). This did, in fact, occur and, after a run-in with the Boss–Finance Director, many of the financial controls were jettisoned. The Finance Director and the rest of the Bosses had to manage by the seat of their pants for a while. The advantage to this Juggler company was, however, apparent.

Professional and Attractor

There are also different ways of resolving the Openness issues, as Table 4.7 describes. A Professional resolves the issues of Openness by being low in Openness. An Attractor resolves the issues of Openness by being high in Openness. Being a combination of the two is a very powerful position, or a state of muddle. Most of the Executive Committee in our case study were Professionals; two were Attractors. The bulk of the Attractors in the company tended to be further down the hierarchy. The Executive Committee never really dealt fully with the Openness issues but, if they had, they would have found it relatively easy to

Table 4.7 Professional and Attractor

Professional	*Attractor*
• Likes things cut and dried	• Likes things warm and fluffy
• Do not like to be too open	• Like to be open
• Like to appear professional	• Like to appear friendly
• Cool	• Warm

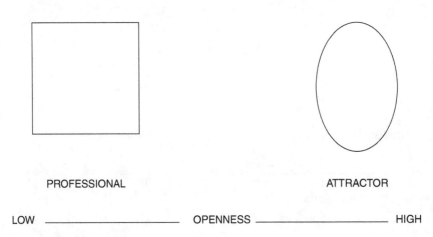

Figure 4.3 Professional and Attractor.

create a culture and practice of Attractor behaviour in the organization as a whole, as Table 4.7 illustrates.

Another client, a small government agency, had a Branch Manager who was a Professional. One of the teams under her command was a team publishing a national encyclopedia. The latter was the most successful part of the Branch but the Branch Manager disliked them. The team had a classic Attractor profile. In the case of this client, the Branch Manager's aversion to the style of the Attractor led her to try to fire them (because they were 'messianic'). My own efforts were to salvage them, to shore them up.

The other Executive Committee

Not all Executive Committees end up circling round and round Control issues. Some end up circling round and round Openness issues. One colleague and I were working for a computer company. Everything we bumped into was an issue of trust. The executive committee agreed to let us take them away for a two-day retreat. This was a first for them; until then they had never let consultants use up their time in this manner. They allowed us to do it because we had been doing a lot of work for them and they knew they could talk to us. The chat we had with the CEO prior to the retreat was the same. This occurred only because he had seen us work and trusted us. The HR director hired me to do a 360 degree feedback on him alone for a similar reason; he trusted me. Those are the positive versions of a trust issue. On the other side of it, the members of the Executive were racked with distrust of each other, of customers, of competitors.

One of the key issues in the organization was empowerment. The issue was not a control one, however. It was because there was a lack of trust that the people in the organization would behave appropriately if the controls weren't there.

Note that, if the issue is treated as one of Control not Openness, the situation might be made worse. People might feel even less trusted than before. One of the guiding principles for using the Inclusion–Control–Openness framework is that you deal with solutions that match the dimension implicated as an issue. If the issue is an Inclusion one, you create Inclusion solutions. If the issue is a Control one you create Control solutions. If the issue is an Openness one you create Openness solutions. In this instance, Openness was where the energy was.

Determining the main dimension

The three dimensions, Inclusion–Control–Openness, need to be all dealt with in some way. They each pose issues or conflict which needs to be resolved. In reality, however, many organizations consider that one of them is a bit more real or important than the other two. In this section we explore how to decipher what that key dimension is for any organization.

A company with Inclusion as its main, most real dimension will have presence in the market, irrespective of its size. When commentary about industry developments is required, they are often asked their opinion. Because of this, their name is known outside its customer base. Distribution channels are vital. Within the organization, cross-organization activities are seen as critical.

Table 4.8 illustrates.

In one company, the bias was the control dimension. How could you tell? The decisive elements were as follows. First was the emphasis on talent. It had very intelligent, clever people that made it stand out from the pack. It was a big organization and much of its stature came from its size. It emphasized strategy including strategic thinking as well as planning. These aspects were real living documents. Further, it measured a lot of things. Most of these facets of the organization were done well. It was also a highly trusted organization but trust was not its primary area. It was mostly trusted because of its size not because of

Table 4.8 The main dimension for an organization

Inclusion	Control	Openness
• Presence in market irrespective of size	• Talent is their key focus	• Culture is the key focus and priority
• Focus on identity of company/team	• Pay great attention to strategy of some sort	• Trust and trustworthiness are watchwords
• Marketing or R&D are key	• Pay great attention to delegation	• Loyalty is taken for guaranteed
• Rely extensively on distribution channels	• Hone their decision making	• Friendships are cultivated
• Cross-organization channels are key	• Often size (small or large) is paramount	• Non-work activities are key

68   *Conflict within organizations – teams*

its innate trustworthiness. Its weakness was the Inclusion dimension. This is so because of the in–out groups inside it; the fact that they were hard to know and it rested on its authority and stature not presence.

The final example, to illustrate a company with Openness as its main dimension, was a company in the retail industry. First, they relied heavily on their company culture and wanted it to be right for the company. Trust was a big issue. Loyalty was also key; they were a long-stay company. Friendships and non-work activities were a priority.

Conclusion

The context for our exploration of the Inclusion–Control–Openness theory has been teams within the organization as a whole. Needless to say, this theory can be (and usually is) used at an interpersonal and individual level. I have at times strayed beyond the original boundaries defining this chapter. This merely emphasizes the fluidity of the People Models. In the next section, I try to describe these dimensions by analysing Sir Alex Ferguson, mega-famous ex-football manager of Manchester United. Now retired from that, he gives us a live way of 'seeing' the Inclusion–Control–Openness model. It is helpful that he has pretty much sorted out the conflicts of each dimension. He seems to be, overall, a Connoisseur.

In the next chapter, we move on to Interpersonal conflict, exploring the Gestalt Cycle of Experience

Case study: Sir Alex Ferguson

In this case study I move from applying the Inclusion–Control–Openness model to teams, to applying it to one individual. The dynamics of the model are the same. Sir Alex Ferguson is renowned as a football manager, stayed at Manchester United as manager for a very successful 23 years, winning many championships in that time.

In order to analyse him I have taken quotes from two of his books (Ferguson, 2013, 2015). These are simply a sample of comments: his preferences are quite clear on the Inclusion–Control–Openness model and are Connoisseur for the Inclusion dimension, Boss for the Control dimension and Attractor for the Openness dimension. He learns over time to add some Juggler for the Control dimension, and to add some Professional for the Openness dimension.

Commentary 4.1 describes his comments relevant to the Connoisseur and Populist.

Commentary 4.2 describes the comments relevant to the Juggler/Boss dimension.

Commentary 4.3 sets out the comments for the Attractor not the Professional.

Commentary 4.1 Sir Alex Ferguson: Connoisseur not Populist

Connoisseur not Populist	*Commentary*
"I could not help but think that the quieter ones [this is at Harvard Business School], who seemed to be absorbing everything, were the people who would become most successful" (Ferguson, 2015, p. 2)	The first two quotes illustrate the inner workings of a Connoisseur. Trying to identify 'quality' can be observed in the first quote. To a Connoisseur, they will respond to quiet more than noise.
"I wanted to separate myself. I don't know why. To this day I don't know why I did that. I had to be on my own … I had to escape into my own wee vacuum" (Ferguson, 2013, pp. 31–32)	Needing to escape into your own world/ vacuum is part and parcel of the Connoisseur.
"The minute that we don't work harder than the other team, we'll not be Manchester United" "And what I would say to anyone whose confidence was wavering is that we were Manchester United and we simply could not allow ourselves to drop to the level of other teams" (Ferguson, 2013, p. 253)	The next two quotes focus on issues of identity (an Inclusion issue). They are indicative of the Inclusion issues and conflict being resolved. They focus on the individual fitting into the team.
"Our whole reason for being was to make sure all the pieces of our product – all the different players – fitted together" (Ferguson, 2015, p. 61) "People try to apply to football the usual principles of business. But it's not a lathe, it's not a milling machine, it's a collection of human beings. That's the difference" (Ferguson, 2013, p. 60)	He is preoccupied, in both books, with describing individual players in great depth but then he also spends time building them into a team. Fitting the players together. This is the Inclusion conundrum being resolved. His job has something to do with creating something out of a 'collection of human beings'.

70   *Conflict within organizations – teams*

Commentary 4.2 Sir Alex Ferguson: Boss not Juggler

Boss not Juggler	*Commentary*
"The one thing I could never allow was loss of control, because control was my only saviour" (Ferguson, 2013, p. 131)	Here we have a very clear high control Boss. There is only one boss and that's him.
"You have big players, wealthy players, world-famous players and you have to rule over them, stay on top of them. There is only one boss of Manchester United and that's the manager" (Ferguson, 2013, p. 200)	
"I placed discipline above all else" (Ferguson, 2015, p. 35)	
"I never expected the players to love me, but neither did I want them to hate me.... All I wanted was for them to respect me and follow my instructions" (Ferguson, 2015, p. 121)	
"Someone says to him 'I never see you smile during a game'. His reply is 'I'm not there to smile, I'm there to win the match'" (Ferguson 2013, p. 7)	The competitiveness (being there to win the match) is also a control dimension expression.
"[My assistant manager] sat me down and asked me why I had hired him. The question perplexed me until he explained that he had nothing to do since I insisted on doing everything. [Sir Alex Ferguson adapted his approach and spent more time on the side lines of a training session, watching and supervising.] It was the most important decision I ever made about the way I managed and led [being a step removed from the fray]" (Ferguson, 2015, p. 17)	The second-to-last quote, about his assistant manager, describes him leading in a more Juggler manner. The game of football itself is more Juggler than Boss but that doesn't mean you need to manage it as a Juggler.
"The longer I stayed the further I looked ahead. Regeneration was an everyday plan" (Ferguson, 2013, p. 241)	The control conflict is resolved with the last quote concerning regeneration and looking further ahead, every day. This is a combination of the Boss and the Juggler.

Conflict within organizations – teams 71

Commentary 4.3 Sir Alex Ferguson: Attractor not Professional

Attractor not Professional	*Commentary*
"Having a quick temper helped [in his early years with Man United] because if I lost my rag my personality came through … [My temper] was a useful tool" (Ferguson, 2013, p. 27) "I had some terrible mood-storms and I was never proud of my outbursts" (Ferguson, 2013, p. 131)	This is an interesting dimension. He is certainly not a buttoned-down Professional although he does learn to become more of one over time when relating to the media. The Openness dimension is about being open and he is so even when losing his temper.
"Faced with the need to confront a player who had performed below our expectation, I might have said: 'That was rubbish, that'. But then I might have [followed it up] with 'For a player of your ability'" (Ferguson, 2013, p. 253)	This kind of feedback (softening the blow) is also indicative of the Attractor.
"In order to build trust and loyalty with the players, I had to give it to them first. That is the starting point for the bond on which great institutions thrive" (Ferguson, 2013, p. xi)	The most interesting quote is the last one, about giving trust first if you want it back. This is a lesson hard-learned by many people who want to give trust only after they have received it. Doing it Sir Alex Ferguson's way is the way to resolve the conflict and issues of the Openness dimension.

Exercises

1 What phase of team development do you think your team/project team is in? Why do you think that?
2 What phase of team development do you think the senior team is in? Why do you think that?
3 What is the most dominant one of the dimensions in your organization? Inclusion, Control or Openness?
4 What is your own strongest dimension?
5 What does the fundamental conflict of the Inclusion dimension mean to you?
6 What does the fundamental conflict of the Control dimension mean to you?
7 What does the fundamental conflict of the Openness dimension mean to you?
8 How can you use the Inclusion–Control–Openness theory to resolve conflict in your organization?
9 Is that conflict relating to the Inclusion, Control or Openness dimension?
10 How do you know?

Checklist 4.1 Connoisseur or Populist

In the continua below, mark each row from 1 to 7. A '1' in the first dichotomy means the organization is maximum reflective. A score of '7' would mean the organization is maximum participative. The two ends (reflective and participative) are not always logically opposite. They are psychologically opposite. There is no good or bad, better or worse associated with any of the scores. A score of 1 does not mean inadequacy. We are simply weighing up apples and oranges.

Key qualities that define the organization

Connoisseur 1............2............3............4............5............6............7 Populist

Reflective ....Participative

Individualistic .... Group-oriented

Distinctive...Diverse

Dignified ....Jovial

Interesting .... Entertaining

Innovative .... Modernizing

Stylish ....Current

Total =

(The maximum Connoisseur score is 7; the maximum Populist score is 49. A mid-range score is, then, 28.)

Values and assumptions about work practices

Connoisseur 1............2............3............4............5............6............7 Populist

Can work alone .... Belong to a group

Value specialists... Value all-rounders

Have own view ....Find consensus

OK to be different .... OK to be popular

Best to reflect first ....Best to act first

Separate space .... Open planning

Originality rewarded ....Energy rewarded

Total =

(The maximum Connoisseur is 7; the maximum Populists score is 49. A mid-range score is, then, 28.)

Copyright material from Annamaria Garden (2018), *How to Resolve Conflict in Organizations*, Routledge

Checklist 4.2 Juggler or Boss

In the continua below, mark each row from 1 to 7. A '1' in the first dichotomy means the organization is maximum adventurous. A score of '7' would mean the organization is maximum careful. The two ends (adventurous and careful) are not always logically opposite. They are psychologically opposite. There is no good or bad, better or worse associated with any of the scores. A score of 1 does not mean inadequacy. We are simply weighing up apples and oranges.

Key qualities that define the organization

Juggler 1................2................3................4................5................6................7 Boss

Adventurous..Careful

Free ....Powerful

Agile...Strategic

Streetwise...Informed

Experimental..Directed

Challenging..Assured

Resourceful..Prepared

Total =

(The maximum Juggler score is 7; the maximum Boss score is 49. A mid-range score is, then, 28.)

Values and assumptions about work practices

Juggler 1................2................3................4................5................6................7 Boss

OK to change routine..Regular routine

Start before planned..Always plan first

Find out yourself..Find out direction

Experiment...Follow plan

Be flexible..Be in control

Reward independence...Reward reliability

Procedures ignored...Procedures used

Total =

(The maximum Juggler score is 7; the maximum Boss score is 49. A mid-range score is, then, 28.)

Copyright material from Annamaria Garden (2018), *How to Resolve Conflict in Organizations*, Routledge

Checklist 4.3 Professional or Attractor

In the continua below, mark each row from 1 to 7. A '1' in the first dichotomy means the organization is maximum serious. A score of '7' would mean the organization is maximum generous. The two ends (serious and generous) are not always logically opposite. They are psychologically opposite. There is no good or bad, better or worse associated with any of the scores. A score of 1 does not mean inadequacy. We are simply weighing up apples and oranges.

Key qualities that define the organization

Professional 1............2............3............4............5............6............7 Attractor

Serious..Generous

Well-presented..Natural

Professional..Spontaneous

Calm..Expressive

Private...Personal

Cautious...Revealing

Polite...Kind

Total =

(The maximum Professional score is 7; the maximum Attractor score is 49. A mid-range score is, then, 28.)

Values and assumptions about work practices

Professional 1............2............3............4............5............6............7 Attractor

Should stay on task..Could get off task

Streamline work..Enjoy work

Appearances matter..Should be human

Efficiency..Friendliness

Rely on e-mail, phone..Rely on face-to-face

Best to be professional..Best to be genuine

Prioritize ability..Prioritize integrity

Total =

(The maximum Professional score is 7; the maximum Attractor score is 49. A mid-range score is, then, 28.)

Copyright material from Annamaria Garden (2018), *How to Resolve Conflict in Organizations*, Routledge

Checklist 4.4 How well does your organization meet Inclusion issues?

The aspects below indicate how well any organization (or part of it) is solving the Inclusion issues it is faced with. You can rate each aspect on a scale of 1–7 (low to high).

Aspect	Rate from 1–7
1. The organization has a clear identity to others. People know what it is like not just what it does.	
2. The organization can claim attention when it wants to without having to grab attention (from customers and employees, alliances).	
3. The organization is good at working in teams; encouraging each individual to be unique and also participate as a team member.	
4. The organization is at ease interacting with other organizations (media, government, alliances, competitors).	
5. The organization is able to go its own way without following the current fads in the industry.	
6. The organization can balance the priorities of R&D or design with marketing.	
7. People feel they have a right to exist in this organization.	

Total out of 49 =

Overall, how well do you think the organization is functioning with Inclusion issues?

Copyright material from Annamaria Garden (2018), *How to Resolve Conflict in Organizations*, Routledge

Checklist 4.5 How well does your organization meet Control issues?

The aspects below indicate how well any organization (or part of it) is solving the Control issues it is faced with. You can rate each aspect on a scale of 1–7 (low to high).

Aspect	Rate from 1–7
1. The organization is effective at achieving the goals it sets itself.	
2. The organization is comfortable with power without either avoiding its expression (and, therefore, abdicating), or without abusing power and being unnecessarily forceful.	
3. The organization has self-confidence not simply from education but from the awareness that whatever it is faced with, it will be dealt with, with no excuses.	
4. The organization is able to easily release the talent in the organization.	
5. The organization can both plan ahead and change plan instantly and regenerate itself in the process.	
6. The organization can combine spontaneity and control.	
7. The organization is able to gain the resources it needs as well as be resourceful with them, not wasting them.	

Total out of 49 =

Overall, how well do you think the organization is functioning with Control issues?

Copyright material from Annamaria Garden (2018), *How to Resolve Conflict in Organizations*, Routledge

Checklist 4.6 How well does your organization meet Openness issues?

The aspects below indicate how well any organization (or part of it) is solving the Openness issues it is faced with. You can rate each aspect on a scale of 1–7 (low to high).

Aspect	Rate from 1–7
1. The organization is good at creating good relationships whether inside or outside the organization.	
2. The organization creates loyalty inside and outside the organization; people want the organization to do well.	
3. Customers and alliances stay with the organization out of choice not because they have been contracted to.	
4. The organization makes genuine contact with people.	
5. The organization is easily able to get others to believe in it and what it is doing.	
6. The organization engages genuinely with its tasks; people truly fix problems rather than papering over them.	
7. The organization gives first (e.g. trusts others first) without waiting to see that they are given to first.	

Total out of 49 =

Overall, how well do you think the organization is functioning with Openness issues?

Copyright material from Annamaria Garden (2018), *How to Resolve Conflict in Organizations*, Routledge

78   *Conflict within organizations – teams*

References

Chun, J. S. and Choi, J. N. (2014). Members' needs, intragroup conflict and group performance. *Journal of Applied Psychology*, 99, 3, 43–45.

De Wit, F. R., Greer, L. L. and Jehn, K. A. (2012). The paradox of intra-group conflict: a meta-analysis. *Journal of Applied Psychology*, 97, 2, 360–390.

Ferguson, A. (2013). *My autobiography*. London, UK. Hodder & Stoughton.

Ferguson, A. (2015). *Leading*. London, UK. Hodder & Stoughton.

Garden, A. (2000). *Reading the mind of the organization*. Aldershot, UK. Gower Publishing Limited.

Garden, A. (2015). *Roles in organization development*. Aldershot, UK. Gower Publishing Limited.

Garden, A. (2017). *Organizational change in practice*. Oxford, UK. Routledge.

Jehn, K. A. and Mannix, E. A. (2012). The dynamic nature of conflict: a longitudinal study of intragroup conflict and group performance. *Academy of Management Journal*, 44, 2, 238–251.

Rico, R., de Latteras, M. A. and Tubernero, C. (2011). Work team effectiveness, a review of research from the last decade (1999–2009). *Psychology in Spain*, 15, 1, 57–79.

Schutz, W. (1984). *The truth option*. Berkeley, CA. Ten Speed Press.

Varela, D. E., Burke, M. J. and Landis, R. S. (2008). A model of emergence and dysfunctional effects of emotional conflict in groups. *Group Dynamics: Theory, Research and Practice*, 12, 2, 112–126.

5 Interpersonal conflict

Projection

I once had an interesting experience in a client of mine in the UK. He was a senior manager, the IT Manager; I have written about him in another context in the Introduction. He was ex-special forces personnel but wasn't, at the time I knew him, really performing. I had had a hand in recruiting him and had misgivings about the wisdom of my advice. He famously did not get on with his boss (who was also my main client in the system). One day, the IT Manager and I were chatting and he started complaining about his boss. He criticized the boss' lack of communication, lack of vision, lack of management skills. Some days later, I was interviewing one of the IT Manager's direct reports. He and, apparently, his colleagues criticized the IT Manager's lack of communication, lack of vision and lack of management skill. I laughed but it wasn't funny.

The IT Director had probably been '*projecting*', a defence mechanism. In other words, blaming another (his boss) for what he was responsible for himself, but wouldn't own or admit to.

This is one of a series of simple interpersonal dynamics which I will characterize as a Gestalt process. Defence mechanisms are not solely the province of Gestalt but, to me, they have relevance from being taught by Professor Ed Nevis (a well-known organizational consultant trained in Gestalt processes) who was on the faculty at MIT.

In this chapter, initially, we will explore defence mechanisms. The main People Model for this chapter, however, is a Gestalt process called the Cycle of Experience. We then explore two modes of influence described by Ed Nevis, Provocative and Evocative. We finish with a case study, this time of a travel company called Flight Centre (FCTG).

Key points in this chapter

Table 5.1 sets out the key points in this chapter.

80 *Interpersonal conflict*

Table 5.1 Key points in this chapter

- Projection
- Key points in this chapter
- Defence mechanisms
- Up the Swiss Alps
- Feedback from the troops
- The Gestalt Cycle of Experience
- Resistance to the Cycle of Experience
- Empowered leadership
- Other interruptions in the Cycle of Experience
- Different modes of dealing with conflict
- Conclusion
- Case study: Flight Centre – FCTG
- Exercises
- Checklists

Other defence mechanisms

Another common defence mechanism used in organizations is '*Deflecting*'. This is described by Polster and Polster as

> a maneouver for turning aside from direct contact with another person.... The heat is taken off by ... excessive language, by laughing off what one says, by not looking at the person one is talking to, by being abstract rather than specific, by not getting the point ... by politeness instead of directness ... by substituting mild emotions for intense ones.... All of these deflections make life watered down. Action is off-target; it is weaker and less effective.
>
> (1973, p. 89)

One of my main clients used Deflection a lot. They avoided issues in general, put things off, avoided people and people-issues. After a long series of Development Centres, for example, which didn't avoid anything, we were faced with the So What question: what were we going to do with these findings?

The latter almost got shelved (which would have been Deflection). However, one Director decided to undertake with me an exercise to draw together all the data and write summary statements for each individual. This was hard to do and took ages but it stopped the company indulging in their usual Deflection.

Other defence mechanisms which reflect interpersonal conflict are: Introjection, Retroflection, and Confluence. Table 5.2 sets them all out (see Polster and Polster, 1973, pp. 70–97).

Confluence

In another client, one manager had been singled out to work on a change programme which was run by external consultants. The context was rather fraught

Table 5.2 Defence mechanisms involved in interpersonal conflict

Defence mechanism	Description
Introjection	Absorbing into oneself wholesale, without consideration, an idea, aim, opinion from someone external to oneself
Retroflection	Doing to oneself what one wants to do to others; or doing to oneself what one wants others to do to you
Confluence	Adapting extremely to others or the environment without considering one's own unique viewpoint or self
Projection	Assigning to others traits, qualities or acts that one has oneself; particularly in criticism
Deflection	Avoiding or ignoring issues that need to be dealt with, particularly in relation to another person

and there were likely to be a certain number of redundancies. I had never liked this manager and the reason is because he was too confluent. I could never get a straight answer out of him as he was always trying to figure out what I wanted him to say. When he joined the change team he became worse. His views became those of the change team. No doubt this was partly due to the threat of redundancies but it was also due to his prior disposition to be confluent.

Introjection

I discovered introjection when I was doing my PhD at MIT (Boston). One day, Professor Ed Nevis introduced me to his wife, Sonja, a leading Gestalt practitioner. I told her about my findings on burnout in management students and occupational health nurses and she said "that's introjection" and explained to me what that meant. There were four themes to my findings. The first I called Boundaries: High burnout people had weaker boundaries between themselves and their work/study. The second theme was Closure: High burnout people had difficulty experiencing closure and had to keep going at something for hours until it was 'finished'. The third theme was Self-Investment: High burnout people invested all of themselves in whatever they were doing. The fourth theme was Self-exploration: High burnout people were more likely to be exploring themselves. All of these themes told Sonja that burnout was a pattern of introjection. The burned out person had absorbed an idea or opinion about themselves or the world, wholesale, without chewing on it (or digesting it), and making it theirs. They were run by something that wasn't truly of themselves.

Retroflection

The best example I can think of concerns me and clothes. When I was a child, I was always given fewer, or less fashionable, clothes than my elder sister. I hated

82   *Interpersonal conflict*

it. By the time I was much older I had turned the situation on its head. I had amassed 26 suitcases worth of clothes and seven wardrobes full of shoes. I was doing to myself what I had wanted done to me. That is retroflection!

Defence mechanisms are common in conflict and it is worth bearing them in mind when engaged in trying to resolve conflict. They can arise from inner conflict (see Chapter 6) as well as interaction with others (this chapter).

However, they are not all there is to understanding interpersonal conflict. The focus of this chapter is on a concept called the Gestalt Cycle of Experience. This next story uses this concept to explain a series of events and unravel why conflict occurred.

Up the Swiss Alps

Step one of the People Procedure: background and context

In Chapter 4 I described briefly a course I taught at IMD, the Swiss management school in Lausanne. This was in the context of a team that had worked through Openness issues and was really humming. We were to be in Lausanne for two weeks but, in the intervening Friday to Sunday we would be in the Swiss Alps. Nobody knew what we would do there except the Director of the programme. In the prior week I did my job of melding my group. On the Friday I was assigned the role of dumb driver: I was to receive instructions on where and how to drive, and then drive, but otherwise I was not allowed to speak, grimace or laugh. My group had to work out where to go in the Swiss Alps. As I drove, we came to a pretty, quiet Swiss village. My group unanimously decided to take a 'tourist' break in this village, asked me to stop and ran around taking photographs. I admired them for taking such initiative and thought it was hugely funny. After an hour, they remembered they were on their way to a destination about one to two hours away, from their interpretation of their instructions. What the Programme Director would have to say to us didn't bear thinking about. I got in the driver's seat, delighted with my group, and we took off. Eventually, we found the destination. The Programme Director was furious when I explained that the group didn't get lost but had taken a tourist break. We were ordered to our quarters.

The next day was spent abseiling, walking along cliff faces and jumping off a bridge backwards. I decided to participate in all of this as I reasoned that if my group had to do it, so should I.

Towards the end of the day, we finished with a boat race (already described in Chapter 4) which my group won. There was a very serious consequence to our winning the boat race because the team who won was split in two and had to lead half of the other remaining groups in an exercise the following day. My team had to work through the night getting everything ready. The other groups were free to chat and relax all night. In other words, by tomorrow there would be two large groups, each run/led by half of my group. The management exercise would take seven to eight hours. Most importantly, the two groups would compete with each other. For my team, well-bonded, this was excruciating. They were fighting against their friends and took hours to get into a proper mode of thinking.

The next day dawned, beautiful and sunny. The two CEOs (chosen the night before from my group) started their assigned teams in different places and they were off. That was the only similarity during the entire day even though their task was exactly the same: each large team had to build an object, the same shape and properties, with the same parts. Those parts were hidden around the lake and among the trees and had to be found. There were various restrictions around how they found those parts, and how to put them together to make the object.

However, the two groups couldn't have done the exercise in a more different fashion if they tried. This was largely due to the towering personalities of the two CEOs. They were both highly competent managers with diametrically opposite styles. One was an entrepreneur with his own very successful business. The other was a successful engineering manager. The former gave minimal instructions to anyone. His direct reports responded likewise and gave very few instructions to anyone. They did, however, share freely the bits of paper with the instructions they received from us (the facilitators). There were few lines of authority or assigned roles. The CEO was enthusiastic on top of utter chaos and confusion. Everyone moaned from beginning to the end of this day. However, amidst all the confusion, they assembled the object and won.

The second team, with the engineering manager as CEO, had worked out very organized roles, clear lines of authority; an efficient hierarchy. He had focused on keeping communication flowing, and reporting lines to keep him informed of what people were doing. People moaned but less so, by far, than in the first group. In the end, the group did not find all the available parts of the object in the available time.

The first group won the simulation. None of the troops could conceive that the first group winning had anything to do with the first group's CEO. I could, and here is the explanation as to why that was so.

Feedback from the troops

The feedback from the two groups occurred all together, as one. That for group one dominated the entire two hours. There were no congratulations for the CEO winning the game. His troops were angry: at being left out in the dark for the duration of the simulation; for the mass of confusion; no one had been assigned proper roles; they had many examples of communication gone awry; he was a useless manager; no one should have to work under him. The CEO of the second group fared a lot better but the attacks were still there: poor communication; things were out of control; he wasn't a good enough manager to be in charge of so many people. At least he was miles better than the CEO for group one. On balance, it was the most high-conflict, charged feedback session I had ever been part of.

84 *Interpersonal conflict*

Step two of the People Procedure: the People Model – the Gestalt Cycle of Experience

The explanation why CEO number one won is drawn from the Gestalt Cycle of Experience.

With the feedback given above, there was:

- poor communication
- confusion of roles
- atmosphere was wretched
- culture was to do your own thing
- strategy was borderline
- planning minimal.

This is the explanation: one person mobilized his troops and the other didn't. The former troops were mobilized by being given general tasks, an overall objective and let loose. Their natural competitive instincts took over. They wanted to beat the other team. I heard them say as much. They were mobilized. To achieve the latter will always require the CEO to let it rip, take a leap of faith. The fact that they won had everything to do with the CEO.

The second CEO did not mobilize his team; he instructed them and tried to plan things in detail. In the Gestalt model, he interrupted the proper sequence by going straight from awareness to action, missing mobilization.

The Gestalt Cycle of Experience

The Gestalt Cycle of Experience consists of a series of necessary psychological steps or processes that one needs to go through in sequence (see Nevis, 2001, pp. 1–4):

1 awareness
2 mobilization
3 action
4 contact
5 resolution.

Awareness. This step will be triggered by a person, event, idea, process or object engaging our awareness. We become conscious of the existence of that person, event, idea, process or object.

Mobilization. In this stage, our energies are activated. Period. We might be motivated, excited or keen to engage.

Action. At this point, we act. We actually do something to interact with that person, event, idea, process or object.

Contact. This occurs when we have direct engagement with the person, event, idea, process or object. We succeed in making contact with it. We wrestle with it.

Interpersonal conflict 85

Resolution. This stage occurs when some resolution occurs after making contact, if it occurs! Resolution might not be reached.

This sequence can be used to analyse events in minute detail. Or, it can be used to describe more broad-brush processes such as I am doing in the Swiss Alps.

The Cycle of Experience applied to the simulation was so fraught and full of conflict that it is likely there was an 'interruption' in the Cycle of Experience. The focal point for the latter, as I have explained already, is the sphere of Mobilization. Resistances to completing the cycle of experience are numerous. Table 5.3 illustrates the general idea.

Resistance to the Cycle of Experience

The participants were, for the most part, from large successful organizations in Europe, with many resources. The CEO of group one was not one of these; he was an entrepreneur with his own successful company from another part of the planet. His troops had been given minimal structure or roles. They were acting independently, roaming around. They were confused and frustrated. The confusion combined with the freedom galvanized those who were engaged with the game (i.e. they were mobilized to seek their own solutions. And they did). These managers took things into their own hands. I saw them do it. They let the confusion mobilize them. This is what the entrepreneur expected. He knew from his own experience that his management style was effective. The troops couldn't see this in operation, however. Instead, they saw the lack of what existed in their own very structured, very bureaucratic companies.

The second group did not get mobilized. There were too many roles, rules, plans, structures, all of which were interpreted as correct management practice. (Well they are in bureaucracies but not in freewheeling organizations.) Note that, in terms of the People Model in Chapter 4, group one is a Juggler and group two is a Boss. We are trained to think that the Boss ways are correct.

Group two went straight from Awareness to Action on the cycle of experience, which won't work very well. They were full of lists for actions (To Do lists) but they were not mobilized to throw the proceedings out of the window and sort the game out itself.

Table 5.3 Resistance to the Cycle of Experience

Stage of Cycle of Experience	Resistance
Awareness	Haziness, boredom
Mobilization	Passivity
Action	Can't be bothered
Contact	Avoidance
Resolution	Giving nothing

86 *Interpersonal conflict*

Step three of the People Procedure: proportional or equal

Both groups projected an expectation of superiority on to the two CEOs. This is one reason the criticism was so harsh.

Empowered leadership

Step four of the People Procedure: underlying needs and feelings

My model of the underlying needs in the simulation goes to another People Model; the empowering leadership model of Peter Koestlebaum (2002, p. 204). This consists of three dimensions, all of which together create empowering leadership.

$A \times D \times S$

Autonomy × Direction × Support = empowering leadership

These are the underlying needs that empowering leadership taps into. Autonomy means exactly that: everyone seeks autonomy. Direction means that everyone seeks some direction to go in. Support means they need back-up and some team support. In the simulation these needs were at play.

In other words, the underlying needs, in an empowered situation, are to have autonomy – space to do their own thing. Group one had this and group two did not. They needed also a bit of direction, or goal setting. They didn't need detailed instructions. Group one got half of this and group two got half of this right. The former were provided with a bit of overall direction and the second group were provided with too-precise direction. They both needed support, especially from fellow team members. Both groups had some of this; they were convivial and supportive to each other up to a point.

Step five of the People Procedure: dominant theme

The dominant theme was confusion and conflict leading to mobilization but subsequent blaming for the confusion. The impact that group two CEO had on his counterpart was zero. The impact group one CEO had on his counterpart was to assure the latter that his management style was on the right track even though it wasn't.

Step six of the People Procedure: did they want a solution?

They all fervently wanted a solution.

Step seven of the People Procedure: resolution

The right team won.

Other interruptions in the Cycle of Experience

Awareness

One client, where the primary interruption was Awareness, is featured in Chapter 4. The Executive Committee never met as a team and made decisions that impacted other members with gay abandon. In addition, what they were unaware of was their extreme distance to the senior managers (their direct reports) who worked in another location. One of the latter referred to the Executive Committee as being in a space ship miles away from earth and they had forgotten to pre-arrange any communication equipment with earth. Once this fact had been *brought to the attention* of the Committee they all began regular visits to the other location. The visits remained from then on. A lot of good came out of them. This was positive use of the Awareness stage of the Cycle of Experience.

In general, a consultant's bag of tricks rests largely on activating the awareness of the client.

Mobilization

The example of this is in the Swiss Alps.

Action

I lived with the phenomenon of interruption of Action when I worked for four years in a government bureaucracy. I saw over and over people who put up barriers to acting. They used to get frustrated with other people and not realize they were doing the same thing themselves. The weakness in the public sector was lack of Action, not lack of Contact, not lack of Awareness.

I saw another perfect example of lack of action in a client for whom I was doing a Personal Development Plan in a finance company in the City. He was a very senior Budget Manager and had no desire to be promoted higher because of the tasks he would have to do in that position. His feedback from a 360 degree feedback, as well as comments from his boss, indicated displeasure at his lack of action in general in the company. My own thrust was to get him to take action steps as a result of the feedback I was giving him. He struggled mightily with it. I ended up giving him to do lists of things he had to do before my next visit.

Contact

In our last chapter, we explored conflict in teams. Note that the Finance Director as well as another Director were both members of that Executive Committee. They could be classified in terms of the People Models as follows (Table 5.4).

In other words, the two were identical on all the People Models so far. Yet their behaviour was different and they experienced a high degree of interpersonal conflict. In reality, this kind of phenomenon is rare. If there is a great deal of interpersonal conflict there is usually a difference in one or more of their

88 *Interpersonal conflict*

Table 5.4 The two Directors

People Model	Finance Director	Another Director
Partner–Ally–Friend	Ally	Ally
MBTI	ISTJ	ISTJ
Inclusion–Control–Openness	Control dominant: Boss	Control dominant: Boss

profiles on a People Model. (It is also the case that every ISTJ is different from every other ISTJ in the universe.)

Nevertheless, the perspective we have unfolded in this chapter does explain the difference between the two. The Finance Director mobilized other people but the other Director did not. The latter went straight from Awareness to Action. The Finance Director's weakness, on the other hand, was the area between Action and Resolution; in other words, making Contact. He moved along the continuum easily to Contact. Moreover, his actions did not always resolve issues. This frustrated him. Why is this occurring? Because his actions weren't precise enough; didn't hit the bull's eye enough. He took too many actions and needed to focus more and make sure his intent was met (missing contact).

An example of contact occurring without interruption was with a client for whom I was doing a Personal Development Plan (PDP) in a company that existed throughout the globe but its head office was in the City of London. This person was extremely intelligent and admired. However, he was also feared and disliked because he was so arrogant and acted superior to everyone else except a few people more senior to him in the hierarchy. I was tasked with getting this message across to him. Without change from him in this respect, his career would stall although no one would be likely to tell him why. I had to tell him why. I sussed him out in our first session. Then I made up my mind we would tackle this issue head on (make contact) in the next session. My solution was to tell him he was perceived as arrogant and that I had seen it in his behaviour in the previous session. He gulped, breathed in and out and then said, "Is that so?" I said "yes, that is so". "How do I get out of it, then?" was all I got back. We proceeded to work out answers to his question. He was devoted to me for a year afterwards, until I went to live in the US for a while. To have mushied around this issue would have been to not make contact.

Resolution

Resolution does not always occur. Certain things, events, can stay in circulation for years and never be resolved. I have one incident that, for me, has never been resolved. This occurred when I was the President of the British Association of Psychological Type (BAPT) and at loggerheads with another Director. I, and the Board, were spending furious numbers of hours at work trying to build the organization up and get it on its feet. We all did our time on it. I was also chairing the project that set up the first conference for BAPT. The Director would shirk from duties. In one instance she avoided a Board meeting by saying she was running a workshop. However, one of her colleagues told me she was taking a break in the country. I fumed and fumed as I was exhausted. Lying was taboo to me. This incident has interfered with every encounter I have ever had with her and is now so old and far away I doubt if I will ever resolve it.

Different modes of dealing with conflict

The third conflict concept that is part of Gestalt has been described by Ed Nevis as Provocative and Evocative modes of influence (2001). These can also be treated as ways of dealing with conflict.

Awareness of one's own immediate experience and the ability to use it in the here and now with the other person become key skills. To resolve conflict means acting upon one's observations, values, feelings in order to have an effect on another person.

Provocative and Evocative modes of influence

Ed has described the two as follows:

> The provocative mode of influence draws on a belief that system outcomes are what count if one is to be influential, and that nothing of real consequence can occur unless the intervenor causes, or forces, something to happen. Strong actions are taken that are designed to jolt, or intrude upon, the other person's awareness so that the interaction moves rapidly to produce action in response.
>
> In the evocative mode, one strives to get the other person interested in what one is doing, what is being attended to, and what the process being used is. To evoke means to bring about a shift in what is being attended to: the goal is fresh awareness and the education of the other person to be more effective in awareness. There is greater willingness to allow the other person's actions to emerge. The aim is for you to be arousing but not unsettling.
>
> (Nevis, 2001, pp. 126–127)

The Provocative mode may be seen as a *forcing* approach: the Evocative mode is best described as an *emergent* approach. Both can be applied with the same person in the same conversation. See Table 5.5.

Table 5.5 Provocative and evocative modes of influence

Evocative	Provocative
Open-ended intentions	Intent is clearly delineated
Behaviour of the other person emerges	Propel other person to act in a particular way
Actions evoke events and things	Actions make something happen

90 *Interpersonal conflict*

Evocative mode of conflict resolution

One client of mine asked me to go to Johannesburg to put his senior management team there through an Empowerment workshop. The issue, the International Director in London told me, was that they were over-controlling and the Managing Director was a Führer. My mission was to transform the latter in one three day workshop!!

I ran the workshops usually with another employee from the client but, since she couldn't make it to South Africa, the International Director himself as well as his International HR Director would be down for the event and they would help run the sessions, so they said. I had a few misgivings about this but agreed. My mistake, as you will see.

Prior to the workshop I sent out a rather large questionnaire to be filled out by all and sundry: customers, bosses, direct reports, colleagues and so on. Before getting the responses back, for they were to be analysed in London, the Personnel Director in Jo'berg rang to say they wanted to do the statistical work. No one had ever asked before and I said no, I needed to analyse it all before the workshop. There were several other instances when he rang to ask various things: no one else had done so from the other workshops.

At last, I was on my flight to South Africa. I went three days before the workshop in order to meet the Managing Director, the Personnel Director and the top team. They were all predictably polite and I learned very little that way (direct interview).

When the workshop itself started, they all joined in for the most part, and I got some glimmerings of attention when giving them their feedback from the questionnaire. However, when the International HR Director stood up and taught, there was shuffling, staring around the room and very little debate or response from anything she said. We carried on like this for a day. On the second day, the International Director himself turned up. Things went from bad to worse. The South African MD was obsequious. The rest split themselves being polite. But there was no response by them to the workshop agenda. I thought the whole thing was a waste of time. One of the managers had a gun in his pocket the whole time, which unnerved me. He didn't need it in the high-security complex we were in but insisted on it. It became clear when I went around the syndicate groups for a session they were reacting by over-controlling. One of the groups was very intent (mobilized) on sorting out some good action steps to put into practice after the workshop. I was thrilled. They said they didn't want to discuss these things in front of the International Director or the HR Director because they would "tell me what to do", and "hold our hands to the flame". I was not to tell either of them what they had decided in their action steps. I agreed and after coming across other syndicate groups doing the same thing, accepted that we would have a different kind of workshop from the one I had planned. In the main group, I did not process out the discussion in the small syndicate groups. We simply talked about other things. The International Director was furious with them and me because so little was discussed with real meat to it, in the large group. Otherwise everyone clammed up. A day after the workshop the South African Personnel Director took me to lunch and we discussed what had happened on the workshop. The International Director and Human Resources Director should simply never have been on it.

At the end of the workshop the International Director called me to his hotel room. He had ordered some food from room service and, when it came, sat and ate it in front of me. I thought he was immeasurably rude. He asked me how I thought the workshop went and I told him it was fine; they had been working out actions by themselves. He didn't believe me until several months had passed and he had been back to South Africa himself and he saw the changes some of the managers had made, and the efforts the Managing Director had made to not be a Führer any more.

The Evocative mode of influence here

The above has been written with key pieces of People Data, or psychological data, sprinkled through it, which is exactly what happens in real life. The key pieces are as follows:

- questionnaires; they didn't want me to be in control of them
- workshop stalled when the two from HQ came
- no action steps in main group
- little discussion in main group
- MD was obsequious to the International Director
- eating in front of me by the International Director.

The key conclusion was:

- They were interrupting the Gestalt Cycle of Experience at 'action'.

The workshop ended as a partial success mainly because I let things happen and didn't try to control it (Evocative mode). I adapted to them and their idiosyncrasies. Attempting a Provocative mode of influence would have been hopeless; they would have clammed up completely. In the next example, of the Provocative mode of influence, the style is completely different.

The Provocative mode of conflict resolution

In one client, a series of programmes for the top 200 managers was run by me and two others. The programmes were designed so that the intact work team, consisting of a manager and their direct reports were to determine a series of actions that would meet the strategic intent. After a few months, the bulk of activity in the company as a whole, stemmed from one workgroup and a series of interactions the consultants had with them on the workshop, which equated to Provocative influence.

One of the first teams was the Finance team, led by the Chief Accountant with his team of accountants and a Business Director. In their break out group,

92 *Interpersonal conflict*

the Finance team had been great. They had worked out a vision of a company that was entrepreneurial. The key to implementing their vision was their own area, Finance. Unless they relaxed the myriad financial controls and strangulation the company would never become as nimble as it needed to be. They worked out what, few, controls they needed.

On the last day of the workshop they all had to do a presentation on what they were going to do to meet the strategic intent. The Finance team had gone back on their original ideas and focused on the need for control and presented a formula for bureaucracy. I was fuming, as were the other two consultants and we challenged them on their retreat. They shut up and sat down. They joined up again as a group during the coffee break and put back together their original entrepreneurial plan. They came back and presented that new plan to the large group, to great acclaim.

The team did, in fact, implement their new plan and many of the old financial controls were jettisoned. The company changed extensively and rapidly.

There is nothing evocative in my behaviour in this example. Nor is there anything evocative in the behaviour of the participants. All the data is up front: it is easy to diagnose. If one wanted to, one could try and figure out the People Models. It is focused on an interruption to the Gestalt Cycle of Experience at the Contact stage. The Finance team had balked at tackling the real problem. They were taking action but, because they were mobilized by fear, avoided dealing with the real issue (which was to create a more entrepreneurial company).

One of my mentors, Professor Dick Beckhard, practised both Provocative as well as Evocative modes of influence. He was much criticized for using the Provocative style which was brilliant when he used it. This criticism occurred because people in the Organization Development profession had various 'rules' they wouldn't admit to but they seemed, to me, to focus on being very namby-pamby. Dick wasn't. He was a magnificent consultant. I was his teaching assistant for a year at MIT and he taught me a lot in that capacity. He held a Consulting Practicum where he brought in his clients. Dick would put a student team in charge of the client interaction and diagnosis and they would sit in the front of the class. Dick would roam around the edges being Evocative, gathering odd bits of data and storing it up, making sense of all sorts of things that the students missed. Almost always, Dick would intervene and be Provocative. He would make a suggestion to the client that was quite direct and confronting. It was always perfect.

Conclusion

The Gestalt Cycle of Experience, defence mechanisms, and the Evocative and Provocative modes of influence form part of a mighty arsenal with which to deal with Interpersonal Conflict. As was apparent, these concepts can be used beyond the boundaries of Interpersonal Conflict. In the next section we explore a case study of Flight Centre (FCTG) and the process they went through deciding to apply a formula of Family, Village, Tribe to their organizational structure and processes using, unconsciously, the Cycle of Experience.

In the next chapter we move on to inner conflict.

Case study: Flight Centre or FCTG

Flight Centre is one of the world's largest travel groups. It has co-owned operations in 23 countries. It employs more than 19,000 people globally. After starting with one shop in the early 1980s FCTG has enjoyed considerable growth to become a AUS$20 billion business.

I have chosen FCTG as the case study because it seems to get the cycle of experience right. Conflict will occur when a person or organization interrupts the cycle. Frequently, this is at the mobilization stage. Renowned for following the model of Family, Village, Tribe for many years, the next section takes you through the Cycle of Experience of this idea's acceptance. The excerpts come from Johnson (2005, pp. 125–129).

The first excerpt demonstrates the Awareness stage.

> Scroo (the then MD – and now CEO) found the whole concept intriguing not least because the hunter-gatherer reflected much of the practices that Flight Centre already had in place. For example, autonomy and sharing were … characteristic of Flight Centre.
>
> (p. 126)

The simple idea that had caught his fancy was that for most of human history man had been a hunter gatherer. This idea built momentum and then takes shape. This is the mobilization stage.

> What caught the MD's attention … was the way the hunter-gatherer idea could be applied to corporate … [entities] When he discussed the theory with the other partners, they all realised that, the bigger Flight Centre grew, the less it would resemble a hunter-gatherer community. People would become more and more disconnected from the way they inherently preferred to work.
>
> (p. 127)

Next comes the action stage.

> If Flight Centre didn't make some changes to the structure now it was likely that in ten years the whole business would suffer.
>
> (p. 127)

Next is the Contact stage.

> The Flight Centre partners decided to use [Robin Dunbar's figures that the natural size of the human community was 150]. In this way they hoped that as the company got bigger, it would remain adaptable and egalitarian.
>
> (p. 129)

94 *Interpersonal conflict*

Finally, comes the resolution.

> The partners called this operation "Family, Village, Tribe" and began restructuring the company into these units.

> (p. 129)

Exercises

1 What defence mechanism do you use mostly; why do you think you use that one?
2 What defence mechanism does your organization use mostly; why do you think it uses that one?
3 Relate the Cycle of Experience to your own reactions.
4 What stages are you at ease with; what ones do you think you interrupt?
5 Relate the Cycle of Experience to your organization.
6 What stages is it at ease with; what ones do you think it interrupts?
7 Is the Provocative or Evocative mode of influence better? In what way?
8 Which do you use the most?
9 Which does your organization use most?
10 Can you make use of the concept of Family, Village, Tribe?

Checklist 5.1 The Cycle of Experience – Individual

Rate your ability to master each stage in the Cycle of Experience.

Awareness   1(low)..............2..............3..............4..............5..............6..............7(high)

Mobilization   1(low)..............2..............3..............4..............5..............6..............7(high)

Action   1(low)..............2..............3..............4..............5..............6..............7(high)

Contact   1(low)..............2..............3..............4..............5..............6..............7(high)

Resolution   1(low)..............2..............3..............4..............5..............6..............7(high)

How can you improve the lowest scoring area?
How can you strengthen the highest scoring area?

Copyright material from Annamaria Garden (2018), *How to Resolve Conflict in Organizations*, Routledge

Checklist 5.2 The Cycle of Experience – Organization

Rate your organization's ability to master each stage in the Cycle of Experience.

Awareness   1(low).............2.............3.............4.............5.............6.............7(high)

Mobilization   1(low).............2.............3.............4.............5.............6.............7(high)

Action   1(low).............2.............3.............4.............5.............6.............7(high)

Contact   1(low).............2.............3.............4.............5.............6.............7(high)

Resolution   1(low).............2.............3.............4.............5.............6.............7(high)

How can you improve the lowest scoring area?
How can you strengthen the highest scoring area?

Copyright material from Annamaria Garden (2018), *How to Resolve Conflict in Organizations*, Routledge

References

Johnson, M. (2005). *Family, village, tribe: the evolution of Flight Centre.* Sydney, Australia. William Heinemann.

Koestlebaum, P. (2002). *Leadership: the inner side of greatness.* San Francisco, CA. Jossey-Bass.

Nevis, E. (2001). *Organizational consulting: a gestalt approach.* Cambridge, MA. Gestalt Press.

Polster, E. and Polster, M. (1973). *Gestalt therapy integrated: contours of theory and practice.* New York, NY. Vintage Books.

6 Inner conflicts

Detecting inner conflict

To help us through the realms of inner conflict in this chapter, I am using Carl Jung's theories (1969, 1960, 1966, 1971). We look at detecting inner conflict in someone else. But, how can you detect this in another person? In yourself? There is no fool-proof answer. In what follows I tell you about people for whom I perceived inner conflict and I explain what I thought that consisted of.

Inner conflict means more than simply a difference within oneself. It means an active disagreement. Tension. A difference that matters. A serious inner dispute. This is explored in the anecdotes. Sometimes this type of conflict arises in a constructive way: when developing a transcendent function or when moving from the ego to the Self. At other times, these processes are fraught. They can seem straightforward, as for Richard Branson, our case study at the end of the chapter.

Key points in this chapter

Key points in this chapter are described in Table 6.1.

Table 6.1 Key points in this chapter

- Detecting inner conflict
- Key points in this chapter
- The case of the cat
- The People Model: Carl Jung
- Back to the boss
- Balance between conscious and unconscious
- Burnout
- Enantiadromia
- The boss' protégée
- Two Introverted Feeling types
- Individuation
- Conclusion
- Case study: Richard Branson
- Exercises
- Checklist

Inner conflicts 99

The case of the cat

Step one of the People Procedure: background and context

One day, I thought I would be virtuous and started working on a voluntary basis, part-time, at a facility for people with mental health, alcohol and drug issues. I loved the work but not the boss. She was an enthusiastic, charming and effervescent Extraverted Intuitive. (N.B. In her MBTI, she would have been an Extraverted Intuitive Thinking/Feeling Perceiving type.) But she was never anything else. That was one data point. There were several more key data points that I collected together. Second, in a facility like that you are often called to give an account of yourself and your 'journey'. She told exactly the same very flattering story of herself each time. Most people did not. Third, we have the incident of the cat.

Little Nutmeg was my adored friend, my loved companion. As she was to 95 per cent of staff and patients. However, she was 16/17 and was not feeling well. We had been told there was *no* money in the budget for Nutmeg and used to provide her with food ourselves. Going to the vet was taboo. No money. Nevertheless, we took her there and it was decided to put her down. Most of the staff were distraught, except the boss, who didn't actually dislike cats, she was just unfeeling. She brought the subject up at a staff meeting, presumably to get some closure on the incident. However, she misread the mood completely. In the single sentence she uttered over Nutmeg, she was so cold that most of us felt worse; I wished she had said nothing. One of my colleagues was in tears as she asked the boss "What happened to Nutmeg?" The boss said a little and then carried on with the meeting. This was certainly an incident I stored in my back pocket to decipher. In the coffee break, the boss came walking past my table where I sat with my colleague who had cried. The boss glanced at her, saw she was there and proceeded to look up at the ceiling until she had walked passed her and then looked down again. Another data point.

I had known also from the training course I had done with her, in order to do my voluntary job, that she was always talking of being exhausted, went home at night and turned the phone off, didn't answer the door.

Anyone should be able to tell from the outside that there is some kind of inner conflict. I am going to analyse this with the help of Carl Jung.

In the next section, the basics of Jung's typological map as the People Model for this chapter are explained. This overlaps the MBTI map (Chapter 3) but is also clearly different. We then return to my discussion of the boss.

The People Model: Carl Jung

Step two of the People Procedure: the People Model – Carl Jung

The Jungian typological map (1971) describes two attitudes, Extraversion and Introversion, and two pairs of opposite functions, Sensing or Intuition, and

Thinking or Feeling. (Note that in the MBTI, a further axis, the Judging-Perceiving axis, is present.)

Jung 'types' people according to their most developed attitudes and functions. If one is 'typed' Introverted Sensing, this indicates that one has Introversion as the preferred attitude and the most developed (as compared with Extraversion) and Sensing as the preferred and most developed function (as compared with Intuition). The verbal formulation that emerges is, however, just shorthand for the complex interaction of all eight attitudes and functions. The Jungian theory is more complex and more dynamic than the static impression type description conveys. In particular, we need to take into account the role of the unconscious and the theory of opposites. That is what I am doing with my little story about my boss.

An underlying guideline map of the four functions (see Figure 6.1) can be used to illustrate some of the dynamic processes involved. The upper half of the circle is light, representing the conscious side, while the lower half represents the unconscious.

In the diagram, the individual represented would be considered an Intuitive type. Both Intuition and Thinking are associated with the conscious sphere of the psyche. Sensing and Feeling, opposites to the two preferred functions, are shown in the unconscious sphere.

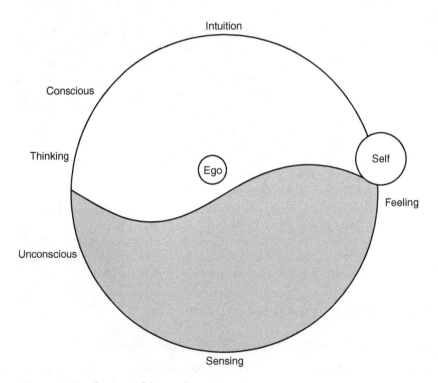

Figure 6.1 Jungian map of the psyche.

For the individual represented in this diagram, there is a further second-order ranking. Intuition is preferred over Thinking which means the former is referred to as the 'dominant' or superior function, while Thinking is the auxiliary or helping function. In other words, the psyche is oriented, first, by the Intuitive function and, second, by the Thinking function.

Jung (1971) tended to assume that only the dominant would be consciously developed and the remainder would tend to be unconscious. Myers (who developed the MBTI) argued that both the dominant and the auxiliary would be developed into the conscious sphere and that the auxiliary balances the dominant. It is one of the main reasons it exists (Myers and Myers, 1980, p. 12). Note that Marie-Louise von Franz (2013) refers to one, two and three functions being developed into the conscious sphere. No one really knows the answers to this conundrum. My own opinion is that Marie-Louise von Franz is correct.

Table 6.2 summarizes very briefly Jung's writing on the eight psychological types. Note that, because there is no Judging-Perceiving dimension in Jung's scheme, we have only eight Jungian types (cf. with 16 MBTI types). He characteristically typed them with reference to the dominant attitude (Extraversion or Introversion) and the dominant function (Thinking or Feeling or Intuition or Sensing).

Table 6.2 Jung's psychological types

Extraverted Intuition	"Its nature is difficult to grasp ... [has] an attitude of expectancy by vision and penetration ... simply transmits images or perceptions of relations between things" (p. 366)
Extraverted Sensing	"no other type can equal the Extraverted Sensing type in realism. His sense for objective facts is extremely developed. His is an accumulation of actual experiences" (p. 363)
Extraverted Thinking	"Is oriented by the object and objective data ... for the [Extraverted Thinking type] the criterion supplied by external conditions is the valid and determining one" (p. 342)
Extraverted Feeling	"follows [his] her feelings as a guide throughout life. [it is] subject to conscious control. [His] her feelings harmonize with objective situations and general values"(p. 356)
Introverted Intuition	"unconscious images acquire the dignity of things ... the Introverted Intuitive moves from image to image, chasing after every possibility in the teeming world of the unconscious" (p. 400)
Introverted Sensing	"is an unconscious disposition which alters the sense-perception at its source, thus depriving it of the character or a purely objective influence" (p. 394)
Introverted Thinking	"at decisive points [Introverted Thinking] is oriented by subjective data.... It formulates questions and creates theories, it opens up new prospects and insights" (p. 380)
Introverted Feeling	"seldom appears on the surface.... It seems to devalue the object.... It is continually seeking an image ... which it has seen in a kind of vision.... It strives after inner intensity" (p. 387)

Source: Jung, 1971, pp. 330–407.

102   *Inner conflicts*

Back to the boss

The boss is likely to be an Extraverted Intuitive, according to Jung's typology. Her auxiliary could be either Thinking or Feeling.

> The Intuitive ... has a keen nose for anything new and in the making. Because he is always seeking out new possibilities, stable conditions suffocate him. He seizes on new objects or situations with great intensity – only to abandon them cold-bloodedly ... as soon as their range is known and no further developments can be divined.
>
> (Jung, 1971, p. 368)

Naturally,

> this attitude holds great dangers, for all too easily the Intuitive may fritter away his life on things and people.... If only he could stay put, he would reap the fruit of his labours; but always he must be running after a possibility.
>
> (p. 369)

Balance between conscious and unconscious

Step three of the People Procedure: proportionate or equal

The inner features of her psyche (at least as far as psychological type is concerned) were seemingly not equal. Her Intuition was dominant, followed by Thinking or Feeling and then Sensing. Her Extraversion was the dominant attitude. However, this may not matter. It is almost definitional that, during development, a dominant Intuition would not be equal to the other functions. Yet, with Jung, the power is all in the unconscious. So, in many ways everything is equalized when one considers the energy that the unconscious functions will have in comparison.

It is considered an integral part of living that each individual will develop one function at the expense of the others, and particularly at the expense of its polar opposite. One must apply oneself to the differentiation of that function with which one is most gifted or which provides the most effective means of ensuring success or survival. The developed functions, and particularly the dominant function, become the means of adapting to and experiencing the world as well as the basis around which to organize one's personality. It is often considered that the facility of the functions is inborn. However, it is possible, for example, to develop most a function which is not the 'naturally' best function. This leads to the development of 'turntypes'.

In spite of this qualification, the more typical development is of the naturally dominant function. While the dominant is being well-developed through receiving a great deal of psychic energy, this is accompanied by a commensurate deprival of energy to the inferior function which remains in the unconscious state and, as such, must be diffused with and permeated by the contents of the rest of the unconscious. Only the conscious functions are capable of direction and subject to the will of the ego since the ego is the centre of the conscious sphere. Since the ego is not the centre of the unconscious, the functions there are not subject to the will and act autonomously.

Subsequent development of the auxiliary and possibly the tertiary functions involves a similar process of 'rising up' from the unconscious to the conscious spheres.

The function which is most developed and the most conscious is the most refined and the most reliable. Each function becomes less able to work as efficiently as the dominant, and more uncomfortable when called upon to be used.

The unconscious functions tend to have a life of their own. They are most often identifiable by their seemingly peculiar, unpredictable and uncontrollable character which to an observer may appear somewhat as an eruption.

Not only does the dominant function become relatively more differentiated, but the ego, as the centre of consciousness, becomes identified with its nature. Thus, an Intuitive will become identified with being creative, insightful, perceptive. A Feeling type will become identified with being caring and concerned with other people. A Thinking type will become identified with being rational and logical; a Sensing type with having his or her feet on the ground, being in touch with reality. One also tends implicitly to assume that this is the way one 'should' be and, moreover, others 'should' be. The mode of the dominant tends to become the 'right' way, the right course to follow in the world, to represent the right ideals and principles of behaviour, etc.

Step four of the People Procedure: underlying needs and feelings

A standard formulation of what is going on with my boss is that she is under a great deal of stress. However, I do not accept that version of events. My version focuses on the inadequate development of her functions, as per the preceding diagram and description.

Put simply, there is too much emphasis on Extraverted Intuition. She needs more psychic balance from Thinking, Feeling or Sensing. The phenomenon is often called 'stress' but it is, in fact, burnout. They are not the same thing.

Burnout

I started reading about burnout during my PhD in order to get myself out of it. I then decided to do my PhD thesis on it (Garden, 1985). Nothing I read really helped, especially the writing and research that had been done in the social services. Because of that I chose two samples: management students and occupational health nurses, one in the human services and one not. My end conclusion was that, while the experience of burnout was negative, the intent of this 'problem' was positive. But I needed Jung's writing to help me sort it out.

104   *Inner conflicts*

So, what is the purpose of burnout? Greater balance in the psyche of the person. During burnout the person's normal means of survival are clumsy and distressed. But the only way out of it is to focus on facets of the person's personality which are opposite to those that the person normally identified him/her self with. The findings can be summarized as follows:

1   Hostility and lack of concern for others was significantly associated with higher levels of burnout only for Feeling types who, by definition, are supposed to have a higher concern for others. Similarly, for Thinking types only, higher levels of burnout were consistently and significantly associated with lower levels of ambition and will to achieve. Theoretically, Thinking types are supposed to show a higher affinity with achievement. For Intuitives, higher levels of burnout were significantly associated with lower levels of enthusiasm and originality, which they are normally identified with. For Sensing types, higher levels of burnout were significantly associated with lower levels of realism and being grounded, which they are normally identified by.

In other words, the character of burnout presented itself as the function being over-used. This looked as in Table 6.3. When burnt out, that character is the opposite of one's 'normal' self.

2   Theoretically, emotional demands should be easier for Feeling types to deal with and mental demands should be easier for Thinking types to deal with. Yet emotional demands predicted energy depletion for Feeling types but not for Thinking types. Similarly, mental demands predicted energy depletion for Thinking types but not for Feeling types. In other words burnout was most strongly associated with the kind of demand each type is naturally adapted to deal with.

Inability to rely on the function which one has been accustomed to use for survival, for adaptation to the environment and for self-identification would in itself be a distressing experience. Getting through each day would be a struggle. All these feelings are frequently described as intrinsic to the burnout experience.

To explain these findings I drew upon a Jungian concept: 'enantiadromia'. This is the emergence of the unconscious opposite in the course of time. This characteristic phenomenon practically always occurs when "an extreme one-sided tendency dominates conscious life" (Jung, 1960, p. 262).

Table 6.3 Over-used functions

Function	Characteristics for that function when high in burnout
Intuition	Lacking in enthusiasm, originality
Sensing	Lacking in realism, and being grounded
Thinking	Lacking in ambition and will to achieve
Feeling	Lacking in concern for others, and hostility

Psychic health is maintained by not living only out of one's conscious functions. The psychic process requires that balance between the conscious and unconscious be maintained. As Jacobi (1963, p. 31) explains, "when the conscious portion of the psyche develops too one-sidedly ... it may easily land itself in a kind of hypertrophy". When this occurs for too long, it will call into action "the self-regulating mechanism of the psyche" (p. 38).

The specialization which occurs via the process of differentiating functions into consciousness at the expense of the functions remaining in the unconscious may occur in varying degrees. Thus, even if Intuition is the superior function, one may still be more or less Intuitive depending on the degree to which that function is differentiated. Similarly, inferior functions can, even if they remain unconscious, have greater or less degree of lack of differentiation (Jung, 1960, p. 419).

Enantiadromia

In general, then, the functions and attitude in the unconscious act as a counterweight. While termed 'opposites' they do not necessarily act in a contrary way to each other. They could represent complementary tendencies. The contents of the conscious sphere can become so developed relative to the unconscious that the latter no longer balances the former but begins to act in opposition to the aims of the conscious ego so that an inevitable tension is produced. This is when the process termed enantiadromia is set off.

If one has been relying too much on, or been identifying too much with, one psychic function and created an imbalance in the psyche, the unconscious may purposively pull the conscious functions down. Too much use of the dominant function would cause, over time, the enantiadromia process. This over-use would only be possible with too many mental demands in a Thinking type. Similarly, with a Feeling type over-use of the Feeling function would be most likely to occur with too many emotional demands. In other words, enantiadromia seems to be part of the burnout process. This is demonstrated further below.

Step five of the People Procedure: dominant theme

The dominant theme for my boss, based on this analysis, is the need for balance in the psyche.

Step six of the People Procedure: does the boss want a solution?

In my view, she did want a solution especially to her exhaustion.

Step seven of the People Procedure: resolution

The only resolution would be characterized by a balance of the psyche by not over-using one conscious function.

106 *Inner conflicts*

The boss' protégée

The mental health facilities boss' favourite employee was, quite simply, disliked by most colleagues. By more colleagues than I have ever encountered in any job. This employee was Extraverted Thinking with a very marked Sensing auxiliary. She was not burnt out but stressed. This is because the environment she was working in was people, and most work demands were Feeling ones, which she abhorred. She wasn't dragging herself through each day (burnout), but was unable to stop herself saying repeatedly how stressed she was. The scenario of her and her boss are in Table 6.4.

While too many mental demands predict burnout for Thinking types, it is too many emotional demands that predict their level of stress. On the other hand, for Feeling types the pattern is reversed. There, too many emotional demands predict burnout but too many mental demands predict stress. In other words, stress, which the protégée was under, arises from dealing with an alien set of demands.

Step one of the People Procedure: background and context

This person was disliked for her overt criticism of everything and everyone. The criticism was self-serving but also established her as a bully par excellence. She was known to be one to every Feeling type in the premises, me included. She was incapable of dealing with Feeling, whether in her colleagues or patients.

Step two of the People Procedure: the People Model – Jung's map of the psyche

This type, the Extraverted Thinking type, is to be found among organizers "[He or she] establishes order by taking a definite stand and saying 'If we say so-and-so, we mean so-and-so'. They put clarifying order into the outer situation" (von Franz, 2013, p. 53). Jung says of them:

> This type of man elevates objective reality, or an objectively oriented intel-lectual formula, into the ruling principle not only for himself but for his whole environment. By this formula good and evil are measured.... Every-thing that agrees with this formula is right, everything that contradicts is wrong, and anything that passes by it indifferently is merely incidental....

Table 6.4 Emotional demands and mental demands

Function	Measure of burnout significantly associated with	Measure of stress significantly associated with
Thinking	Mental demands	Emotional demands
Feeling	Emotional demands	Mental demands

Inner conflicts 107

Just as the extraverted thinking type subordinates himself to his formula, so, for their own good, everybody round him must obey it too, for whoever refuses to obey it is wrong – he is resisting the universal law, and is therefore unreasonable, immoral, and without a conscience.

(1971, pp. 346, 347)

The protégée also seemed to repress Feeling to a large extent. Indeed, it would seem that this function was associated with the shadow. This occurs when any function is actively repressed. Her personality was, therefore, hypercritical, sarcastic, rude and bombastic. She was exactly the same with patients as she was with colleagues. A typical aspect of the inferior function can be its unadaptedness and primitiveness, its touchiness and tyranny. Most people, when their inferior function is in any way touched upon, "become terribly childish" (von Franz, 2013, p. 18).

I once saw her nearly kick our cat, Nutmeg, in the face with kick boxing. She was apparently teasing but the kick landed only an inch or two from the cat's face. The cat was traumatized and so was I. She then proceeded to put the cat outside because it had been naughty; it had been meowing. This behaviour of punishing the cat for meowing was a common occurrence.

Step three of the People Procedure: proportionate or equal

This is an instance where there seems to be an active repression of the inferior function. This implies that there is no equality in the psyche in this person but an active fight against balancing the dominant with the inferior; the conscious with the unconscious.

Step four of the People Procedure: underlying needs and feelings

Her underlying needs are to win the battles in the organization using her superior Thinking function. Thereby she would be seen to have been 'right' while all those ganging up on her would be 'wrong'. I thought at odd times that we needed to take care there was no scapegoating of her going on. However, I became convinced that it wasn't the case.

Step five of the People Procedure: dominant theme

The dominant theme is her bullying behaviour arising from inner conflict.

Step six of the People Procedure: does she want a solution?

She wants her solution, to stay the same, but that is not a resolution of the conflict.

108 *Inner conflicts*

Step seven of the People Procedure: resolution

The resolution is for her to stop repressing her Feeling function and stop over-relying on her Thinking function. This would stop her projections and, ultimately, stop her bullying. She was eventually removed from the facility.

Two Introverted Feeling types

The People Model of Carl Jung does not consist mainly or only of the balance between the conscious and unconscious, or the psychological types. There are also, for example, the enormous concepts of the Self, Individuation and developing a transcendent function. In the anecdotes that follow we look at all of these.

Two clients of mine, both Introverted Feeling, had very different inner conflicts. On the surface, though, they appeared quite similar, as Table 6.5 shows. Both were a Friend in terms of relationship type; INFP on the MBTI; responded most to either the Inclusion or the Openness dimension in Schutz's framework; one had an issue with 'mobilization' and the other on 'contact' on the Gestalt Cycle of Experience.

Introverted Feeling types: the development of functions

Introverted Feeling types

> are mostly silent, inaccessible, hard to understand; often they hide behind a childish or banal mask, and their temperament is inclined to melancholy. They neither shine nor reveal themselves. As they are mainly guided by their subjective feelings, their true motives generally remain hidden. Their outward demeanour is harmonious, inconspicuous, giving an impression of pleasing repose, or of sympathetic response, with no desire to affect others, to impress, influence, or change them in any way ... the truth is [their] feelings are intensive rather than extensive.
>
> (Jung, 1971, pp. 387, 390)

The first client, a female, was Introverted Feeling with a highly developed Thinking function. This, while it must be rare to have the inferior function developed so much, occurred because of pressure from her family, school,

Table 6.5 A tale of two Introverted Feeling types

Introverted Feeling	Introverted Feeling
• Friend	• Friend
• INFP	• INFP
• Inclusion	• Openness
• Mobilization	• Contact
• Introverted Feeling	• Introverted Feeling

university and environment to be a Thinking type not a Feeling type. (On the MBTI she scored equal on the Feeling/Thinking dimension.) She was a 'turn-type'. Even after she had spent ten years wondering if she was really a Thinking type, and then reversing herself: 'maybe she really *was* a Feeling type', could she slowly settle herself into owning the Feeling function and became ostensibly a Feeling type. One of the outcomes of this dichotomy between the two functions was the development of the transcendent function between the two; she could use each equally at the same/similar time. While this battle between Thinking and Feeling was occurring, she developed her auxiliary a lot so it would appear to others that Intuition was the most developed function. However, she was not an Intuitive type. She did develop burnout from focusing only on Intuition so much, while Thinking and Feeling were cancelling each out. At this point, when Intuition had been ruling the roost, she worked consciously at lessening the hold it had on her. The effect was quite marked: it was to slow her down, stop her talking so much and stop her being so Intuitive. Her inferior function wrongly appeared to be Sensing; technically her tertiary. She was oriented primarily to inner adaptation rather than outer adaptation. This means a priority is placed on one's own inner psychic needs especially one's need for psychological development. This is in contrast to adapting to one's own outer needs such as society, work, etc.

She was guided through a lot of this by Ian Gordon-Brown, Director of the Centre for Transpersonal Psychology in London, who had her drawing Jungian maps, imaging, dreaming and talking through the whole confused set-up. She had created her own three principles to live by: be positive, cooperate and succumb.

The other Introverted Feeling type was very pleasant. He was a clear dominant Feeling type and was very Introverted. He cared more about what people thought of him (Persona) than she did. His inferior function was what one would predict: inferior Thinking. However, this had become associated with the shadow as he 'didn't like' Thinking. By shadow, Jung "means the 'negative' side of the personality, the sum of all those unpleasant qualities we like to hide, together with the insufficiently developed functions and contents of the personal unconscious" (1966, p. 66). Over the course of ten years he developed the ability to use his Thinking function very well; to write several books and many articles with a very clear logic to them. He also had developed a transcendent function between Thinking and Feeling.

He was interested in inner psychic work and, initially, was focused on external adaptation. He cared what others thought of him, whether what he did was appropriate. However, he also cared a lot about inner adaptation, increasingly over a ten year period. Most important to him was developing himself spiritually. Table 6.6 illustrates.

Note that a transcendent function arises from the unconscious to meet the demands of both the conscious function (in this case both Feeling), and the unconscious function (in this case both Thinking). It is an integrating function.

110 *Inner conflicts*

Table 6.6 Inner conflicts of two Introverted Feeling types

• Developed thinking even though it was technically the inferior	• Thinking was the inferior function
• Actual tertiary was Sensing	• Thinking was associated with the shadow
• Intuition, the auxiliary, became the most developed	• Intuition was auxiliary; this was well developed
• Over 10 years there was some peace as Feeling became the dominant	• Sensing was his tertiary; no real issues here
• After 10 years had developed a transcendent function, integrating Thinking and Feeling	• After 10 years had developed a transcendent function, integrating Thinking and Feeling
• Inner adaptation	• Inner adaptation

Individuation

Ordinarily, the process of transferring the authority to the Self from the ego is quite tense. It is sometimes allied with the mid-life crisis or period around 40 but not always. One client, a male, struggled for many years to relinquish the certainty and known-feeling of control associated with his ego. What the Self was suggesting/demanding was a transition to an entirely new career, location and lifestyle. He constantly used New Age methods to give himself the illusion of control (that he knew and understood what and why things were happening to him). However, the call to new ways would not be pushed aside for long periods and soon enough he would be faced with these seemingly irrational feelings and dreams leading him away from everything he had built up in his life. He resisted with his ego and eventually he had a complete physical breakdown. This had the effect of withdrawing him from his successful career, income, lifestyle and, eventually, where he lived. It took years to recover. By then he lived in another country and had left behind his career.

Individuation is sometimes thought of as being the same as type development. However, individuation involves something more than the development of the four functions. It involves also a shift in the focal point of the psyche from the ego to the Self. The Self is defined by Jung (1971) as "the unity of the personality as a whole" (p. 460), the centre of the conscious and unconscious spheres. In contrast, the ego is considered to be the "centre of my field of consciousness" (p. 425). Jung himself describes the "almost irresistible compulsion and urge to become what one is. ... This centre [of personality] is not felt or thought of as the ego but, if one may so express it, as the Self" (1969, p. 357).

Further, individuation in Jung's terms is the task not merely of exceptional individuals but of normal individuals too. Jung's view is that type development is a life-long process whereby in midlife "some rare individuals can develop to the point where they transcend their preferences and move easily from one function to another" (p. 301).

Hillman (1972) describes the individuation process and the drive of the Self to be realized as strongly affirming "that this urge to self-realization works with the compulsiveness of an instinct. We are driven to be ourselves, the individuation process is a dynamic, not a matter of choice or for a few" (pp. 34–35).

This process of integrating all the opposite attitudes and functions as well as the shift from ego to Self as the governing centre, is referred to by Jung as self-realization and describes it as "a law of nature" (1969, p. 170).

Hillman (1972) distinguishes two approaches to adaptation. In Jungian terms "adaptation is primarily to psychic reality" (p. 185). As distinct from will and reason, which conceived adaptation "in terms of controlling and understanding reality" (p. 185).

This latter notion of type development achieves only Hillman's second type of adaptation – i.e. meeting the demands of the external situation. It is not a Jungian notion and is opposite to the essential meaning of the individuation process. The latter refers to Hillman's first type of adaptation – i.e. to inner reality, to inner demands. Thus, type development and/or individuation cannot be explained as processes whereby an individual will be able to deal appropriately with different situations.

Conclusion

This chapter has tried to illustrate what is going on with inner conflict. The resolution of these inner conflicts drew partly on my own research looking at burnout and stress which, in turn, was based on Jung's writing and theory. We turn now to a brief case study of moving from ego to Self: Richard Branson.

In the next chapter, we explore the idea of conflict which relates to how we choose to exist, or live a life.

112 *Inner conflicts*

Case study: Richard Branson

My case study in this chapter takes a look at the impact of the Self in Richard Branson, famous entrepreneur originally based in the UK. He has been a budding entrepreneur since 1966 and started the Virgin Group, which controls more than 400 companies. My data for him comes from two of his autobiographies (Branson, 2011, 2014). Commentary 6.1 illustrates.

Commentary 6.1 Richard Branson

Richard Branson quotes from two of his books	*Commentary and interpretation*
"if a new project or business opportunity doesn't excite me and get my entrepreneurial and innovative juices going, if it's not something with which I sense I can make a difference while having a lot of seriously creative fun, then I'd far rather pass on it" (Branson, 2014, p. 1)	He is not just in business to make a profit.
"My actions are always motivated in equal measures by my natural drive to turn old ways of doing things upside down and my insatiable curiosity – indeed, that's how we built Virgin. But, increasingly, what I do is driven by another core goal – to make business a force for good" (Branson, 2011, p. xi)	This passage describes a move from ego to Self (making business a force for good).
"I felt, then, and still do today that every business has enormous potential to be a force for good in the world" (Branson, 2011, p. 273)	He sees this drive as relevant to every business.
"the boundaries between work and higher purpose are merging into one, where doing good really is good for business" (Branson, 2011, p. 1)	Here he refers to a higher purpose: doing good.
"How we protect and harness our natural and human resources is the largest 'great frontier' we will face in our lifetimes" (Branson, 2011, p. xi)	This is the essence of what he is doing.
"as the Virgin Group continues on its journey to transform itself into a force for good for people and for the planet" (Branson, 2011, p. 1)	The transformation is to be good for people and the planet.
"it requires shifting from a narrow focus on short term financial gain to a wider understanding of what it means to make profit" (Branson, 2011, pp. xi–xii)	This is where we started from: life is about more than making a profit.

Exercises

1 Determine what is your dominant function and auxiliary.
2 Are you a turntype in any way?
3 Determine what is your organization's dominant function and auxiliary.
4 Is your organization a turntype in any way?
5 Do you feel you have a balance between your conscious and unconscious?

Inner conflicts 113

6 Are you aware of feeling burnt out? Is your organization burnt out?
7 Are you aware of feeling stressed? Is your organization stressed out?
8 Is there conflict in you that comes from needing to develop your functions?
9 Is there conflict in you that comes from needing to move from your ego to your Self?
10 Is there conflict in your organization that comes from needing to develop the functions, or to move from the ego to the Self?

Checklist 6.1 Development profile

This short profile helps you assess the health of your Jungian attitudes and functions. Rate each attitude and function from 1(too weak) to 7(too strong).

Extraversion 1(too weak)..........2............3............4............5............6............7(too strong)

Introversion 1(too weak)..........2............3............4............5............6............7(too strong)

Sensing 1(too weak)..........2............3............4............5............6............7(too strong)

Intuition 1(too weak)..........2............3............4............5............6............7(too strong)

Thinking 1(too weak)..........2............3............4............5............6............7(too strong)

Feeling 1(too weak)..........2............3............4............5............6............7(too strong)

What is your profile?
Which is higher? Extraversion or Introversion?
Which is higher? Sensing, Intuition, Thinking or Feeling?

Copyright material from Annamaria Garden (2018), *How to Resolve Conflict in Organizations*, Routledge

References

Branson, R. (2011). *Screw business as usual*. London, UK. Virgin Books.

Branson, R. (2014). *The Virgin way*. London, UK. Virgin Books.

Garden, A. (1985). *Burnout: the effect of personality*. Unpublished doctoral dissertation. Massachusetts Institute of Technology. 0373736.

Hillman, J. (1972). *The myth of analysis*. New York, NY. Harper & Row.

Jacobi, J. (1963). *The psychology of C. G. Jung: an introduction*. London, UK. Routledge & Kegan Paul.

Jung, C. G. (1960). *The structure and dynamics of the psyche.* In the Collected Works of C. G. Jung (vol. 18). Bollinger Series, Princeton, NJ. Princeton University Press.

Jung, C. G. (1966). *Two essays on analytical psychology*. In the Collected Works of C. G. Jung (vol. 17). Bollinger Series, Princeton, NJ. Princeton University Press.

Jung, C. G. (1969). *The archetypes and the collective unconscious.* In the Collected Works of C. G. Jung (vol. 9). Part I. London, UK. Routledge & Kegan Paul.

Jung, C. G. (1971). *Psychological types*. In the Collected Works of C. G. Jung (vol. 16). Bollinger Series, Princeton, NJ. Princeton University Press.

Myers, I. B. and Myers, P. B. (1980). *Gifts differing*. Palo Alto, CA. Consulting Psychologists Press.

Von Franz, M.-L. (2013). *Lectures on Jung's typology*. Putnam, CT. Spring Publications.

7 Life conflicts – individual

The effective MD: the power of personality

I had a client once who ran the company more than the real Managing Director (MD), who was largely ineffectual. It meant that the Pretender didn't have the powers of authority but still had influence. You might wonder how he could do this and the answer was in his personality. From what I could see, the factors that enabled him to do what he did were: (a) a penchant for new things. This meant pushing and pulling the organization to be more modern (this was a requirement in this company). (b) He was bright and helpful. The real MD was rather gloomy while the effective MD was quite open and inclusive and people responded very well to this. And (c) he did, however, have a fatal flaw which was that he didn't have a lot of faith in his ability to get things accomplished. This affected his success in his various ventures. All these traits form part of a new People Model which is the basis of this chapter. I illustrate them with three leaders: the CEO of YouTube – Susan Wojcicki; the CEO of Icebreaker – Jeremy Moon; and the Mayor of London – Sadiq Khan. The final case study in this chapter applies this new People Model to Steve Jobs.

Key points in this chapter

Table 7.1 Key points in this chapter

- The effective MD: the power of personality
- Key points in this chapter
- The People Procedure: putting the three states together
- The People Model: Life Conflicts
- Existence
- Susan Wojcicki: CEO of YouTube
- Elevation
- Jeremy Moon: CEO of Icebreaker
- Efficacy
- Sadiq Khan: Mayor of London
- Becoming more good-humoured
- Monitoring the three states
- Organizations and conflict
- Conclusion
- Case study: Steve Jobs
- Exercises
- Checklists

Life conflicts – individual 117

The People Procedure: putting three states together

Step one of the People Procedure: background and context

One of my clients was a medium sized retail company. It was, therefore, a people business. The immediate client I worked for was one of my most difficult clients. They were in a highly competitive market and needed to push through retail-based changes as well as people-based changes on an almost constant basis. The problem was that my immediate client was supposed to be in the fore-front of these requirements as he was the HR Director. One of his colleagues would often have 'a quiet word with me' about him and seek advice on 'how to change him'; 'how to get him on board' with this, that and the other new policy or change. A lot of our discussion focused on how to get him to appear more good humoured.

Our previous People Models have been mostly behavioural. We need one that looks at how to live a life, a framework concerned with states of being not just doing. The People Model in this chapter does exactly that. It relates to both individuals and organizations, as do our previous models, but in this chapter I emphasize the former.

The People Model: Life Conflicts

The Life Conflicts People Model consists of my interpretation and elaboration of the three most useful ideas for living a life, in my eyes, that I have come across. The three components in my model are derivatives, not pretending to be the thing itself. Three original ideas inspired my own model. The first inspiration comes from Victor Frankl, the second from John Haidt and the third from Albert Bandura. There are three sources of innate conflict in this model: no meaning, no sense of being uplifted and no sense of being able to achieve what you set out to achieve. The three positive states that correspond with these conflicted states are Existence, Elevation and Efficacy (note that these names reflect my orientation to the three concepts: for example, Frankl himself refers to 'Meaning', Haidt to Elevation but means something different from my use of the term, and Bandura refers mostly to 'Self-efficacy').

Existence

Existence refers to having a sense of meaning in life and beliefs; but it means also being unique and establishing one's existence easily in the eyes of others. People who are high on this state of being make every moment count and feel fully alive. They relish new things, creating, being first, purpose including spirituality. Checklist 7.1 below is something for you to fill out to gauge your own level of Existence. Low scores (below 25 in total) reflect the fact that you have conflict in this area.

118   *Life conflicts – individual*

Checklist 7.1 Existence in the individual

I am unique; distinctive	1.............2.............3.............4.............5.............6.............7					
I love new things	1.............2.............3.............4.............5.............6.............7					
I am creative	1.............2.............3.............4.............5.............6.............7					
I make every moment count	1.............2.............3.............4.............5.............6.............7					
I feel fully alive	1.............2.............3.............4.............5.............6.............7					
I have a set of beliefs to live by	1.............2.............3.............4.............5.............6.............7					
I have a sense of meaning in my life	1.............2.............3.............4.............5.............6.............7					

Total out of 49 =

Victor Frankl is the inspiration here because of his approach to the need for meaning in our lives. He was an inmate in several German concentration camps in the Second World War. His experiences as a camp inmate led him to discover the importance of finding meaning in all forms of existence and, therefore, a reason to continue living. In this sense, lack of meaning is a paramount existential stress and source of existential conflict. In his form of therapy, logotherapy, people become conscious of the spiritual, or existential (Frankl, 2000).

An example of a person I knew who suffered existential conflict as I am interpreting the term, was a Director of a company in the finance industry. He used to sit in meetings not offering anything to say and then right at the end he would criticize the whole thing. By doing so, he would deaden everything. He didn't like new things. This is the essence of someone suffering existential conflict of this kind, i.e. it is to do with their very existence. He had little meaning in his life except for amassing a huge salary and stocks and shares. He was dispiriting, conventional and what I call a 'withholder'.

An example of a person who escaped this form of conflict was someone who worked in the same company, earned much less but was adored for being a bright spark. He offered advice in meetings, added to things rather than being a withholder. He was on the forefront of whatever was new in the company.

Making emotional sense

In order to illustrate each of the three states, I have used an extract written by one well-known person. These can be interpreted at two levels: the ordinary level of business language and the People Model level of people language. Any statement made by people in business or the public sector must make sense at an emotional level or it will not be interpreted properly by human beings. In the first extract that follows I highlight the words that have particular significance or meaning in the context of the Existence state. It shows the positive or constructive evidence of that dimension. You can use this method to analyse any statement (or advertisement) and get 'under the surface' to see and hear what the author or speaker is really saying.

The first extract we look at illustrates Existence and is written for *The Economist* by the CEO (since 2014) of YouTube, Susan Wojcicki. Commentary 7.1 illustrates.

Susan Wojcicki, CEO of YouTube

Commentary 7.1 Susan Wojcicki

CEO of YouTube	Commentary
"YouTube is **helping** ... build a **new** media economy, where each **creator** acts as their **own** media company....	Notice that YouTube is 'helping' rather than 'making happen'. This is compatible with the new style she is describing. She refers to a 'new media' company; 'creator acts as their own media company', i.e. she is talking about bringing something new into existence as a catalyst.
They do **not seek permission from traditional** media gatekeepers to appear on air; they **create content and share it directly** with their audiences.	This is not a world of 'seeking permission' but of sharing creativity directly with their audience. This is another new way of existing.
And they do not just appear in their videos: they also produce, direct, edit and market them. Though many of them started filming in their **bedrooms**.... Those are the media firms of **tomorrow**.	The newness is in the piece about starting media firms of 'tomorrow' in their 'bedrooms'. This is another facet of creating a new existence.
And they are **creating content** that you could **never find on TV**....	This is a new world being created.
It's clearly a time of **great change** in media but it's also a moment of **great opportunity**. By using **new** technology to give viewers what they are seeking – **more choice** in how they watch and **more options** in what they watch – increasingly we can **empower new voices** and reach **new people across the world**."	She refers to 'great change' and 'great opportunity'. This is the talk of an Existence state. They use 'new' technology, create more choices and options. Ultimately, her larger world view **(purpose in life)** is to '**empower new voices**' and '**reach new people across the world**'. This is the *meaning* in what she does in an Existence state.

Source: *The Economist*. The world in 2017. A new world of watching. January 2017, p. 141. Permission to reprint granted by *The Economist*.

120 *Life conflicts – individual*

Elevation

Elevation is somewhat similar to Martin Seligman's rather broad definition of happiness (2002). However, it is also substantively different. This second key idea is inspired by the writing of Jonathan Haidt around the concept of Elevation. This has been called one of the other-praising emotions along with gratitude and admiration (Algoe and Haidt, 2009). According to Haidt, Elevation occurs as a result of the virtue or skill of others. It is triggered in ourselves by witnessing other's moral beauty (Cox, 2010). However, my version of Elevation is the other way around. It is the (quiet) inward response and sense of surety when *we* perform acts of moral goodness. It is a state of generosity in ourselves without an egotistical component. It is an experience of uplift but with humility not arrogance.

Checklist 7.2 below is something for you to fill out to gauge your own level of Elevation. Low scores (below 25 in total) reflect the fact that you have conflict in this area.

Checklist 7.2 Elevation in the individual

I have a positive nature	1(low)............2............3............4............5............6............7(high)
I like doing the right thing	1(low)............2............3............4............5............6............7(high)
I appreciate moral goodness	1(low)............2............3............4............5............6............7(high)
I am generous	1(low)............2............3............4............5............6............7(high)
I am good-humoured	1(low)............2............3............4............5............6............7(high)
I like doing things for people	1(low)............2............3............4............5............6............7(high)
I focus on relationships	1(low)............2............3............4............5............6............7(high)
Total out of 49 =	

An example of living without Elevation and, therefore, living in conflict was a person I knew who ran a retreat centre which I stayed in several times. Each time she moaned incessantly usually about the staff running the centre. The moaning became predictable and interminable. She used to talk also about the spiritual life and about how people who just search for meaning haven't 'got it'. They needed to search for God she said. In spite of her believing this, she didn't know about the need for Elevation in life as well.

In contrast, a Director of a small business was the opposite. When he walked into the room the lights lit up even before he spoke. He was patient and uplifting. He was simply someone you wanted to know. He was high on Elevation.

Jeremy Moon, CEO of Icebreaker

The second extract we look at illustrates the state of Elevation. Jeremy Moon is a good example of this. He is the founder, in 1994/1995, of Icebreaker, a merino and designer clothing company, and remains CEO of the now global business. It now supplies its clothing to 4700 stores in 50 countries. Commentary 7.2 illustrates.

Commentary 7.2 Jeremy Moon

CEO of Icebreaker	*Commentary*
"In his talk [to scientists and businessmen in Antarctica] Moon discussed the **symbiotic relationship** between business and nature. 'I spoke with a lot of the scientists who find it a challenge to **connect with** the business world, so **I want to see if I can facilitate anything** there and **help be more of a conduit** between some of the science that is happening ... and business applications ... **I love trying to bridge that gap'**....	A person high on Elevation thinks in terms of relationships (here, between business and nature). 'Connect with' is another Elevation phrase. He wants to see if he can 'facilitate' and 'help'; the generosity of the Elevation state. Note the word 'love' trying to bridge that gap. Here, he wants to help others.
'At age 24, Moon **stumbled** across a merino farm and was so **inspired** by the experience that he had to **create** his own garments ... It didn't feel like a risk starting Icebreaker at all. It wasn't a question that lived in my head. **I could feel it in my stomach – it was impulsive'**....	None of this section about starting Icebreaker follows a standard business model. He doesn't analyse the start up but 'feels it in his stomach'.
'It worked because I **spent a lot of time** on merino stations ... I took inspiration from **living within an ecosystem**: this **relationship between the farmers, the environment and the animals**, and understanding how business, in this case a merino station, can be run with a **long run** perspective, **looking after** the animals, looking after the land and making a profit. That for me was probably the choice of inspiration, the business model I have always had in my head'."	Spending 'a lot of **time**' on something is Elevation as is the strategy of 'living within an ecosystem'. The core of his statement is about the **relationships** between the farmers, the environment and the animals. This is Elevation, by definition. Running the business and making a profit comes from '**looking after**' the animals, the land. This is doing the right thing.

Source: *NZ Herald*, 21 January 2017, p. C3. Permission to reprint granted by the *NZ Herald*.

Efficacy

Efficacy is the extent or strength of one's belief in one's own ability to complete tasks and reach goals. Albert Bandura calls this 'self-efficacy' (1977). As indicated, I use the easier term of Efficacy. One's Efficacy can play a major role in how one approaches goals, tasks and challenges. According to Bandura, people with high Efficacy, i.e. those who believe they can perform well, are more likely to view difficult tasks as something to be mastered rather than something to be avoided.

122 *Life conflicts – individual*

Checklist 7.3 is for you to fill out to gauge your own level of Efficacy. Low scores (a total of below 25) reflect the fact that you have conflict in that area.

Checklist 7.3 Efficacy in the individual

I believe I can achieve what I set out to do	1(low)............2............3............4............5............6............7(high)
I set high goals	1(low)............2............3............4............5............6............7(high)
I am efficient	1(low)............2............3............4............5............6............7(high)
I make sure I get done what is needed, no matter what	1(low)............2............3............4............5............6............7(high)
I know what is going on	1(low)............2............3............4............5............6............7(high)
I have deep not shallow confidence	1(low)............2............3............4............5............6............7(high)
I keep momentum going	1(low)............2............3............4............5............6............7(high)

Total out of 49 =

Bandura identifies (1977, p. 191) four factors affecting self-efficacy: (a) the experience of previous mastery, (b) modelling or vicarious experience, (c) direct encouragement and (d) physiological factors such as nerves. If the latter affect your belief in your ability to perform a task that is low Efficacy.

One of the main aspects of Efficacy, in my view of the term, is having deep confidence not shallow confidence. The latter is obtained by, for example, relying on degrees or a fancy education. The former is obtained by making sure you achieve what you set out to, no excuses.

An example of low Efficacy is a senior Director in a manufacturing company. He had a low sense of Efficacy and started many projects but half-heartedly because he didn't think they would work i.e. achieve their aim. His excuse was that he didn't try or put enough effort into things and that was why they didn't work. In this way he avoided facing his low Efficacy state.

An example of high Efficacy is an entrepreneur I know with three to four different sources of activity, each one of which would take someone of lower Efficacy full-time to do. He reminds me of someone spinning plates at the same time and none of them fall. He makes millions but that wasn't the point of what he did. He is having fun and doesn't know how else to use himself fully. He has complete belief that he will achieve what he sets out to achieve. He has never owned or worn a suit or a tie in his life. He never got a degree.

Life conflicts – individual 123

Finally, we come to Efficacy exemplified by Sadiq Khan, the Mayor of London. In his statement, which is almost entirely an Efficacy one, we see what can be achieved by cities. Commentary 7.3 illustrates.

Sadiq Khan, Mayor of London

Commentary 7.3 Sadiq Khan

Sadiq Khan	Commentary
"As Mayor of one of just a handful of truly global cities, I've seen first hand that big cities **are assuming an even greater role** in our globalised world.	'Assuming an even greater role' implies an assumption of Efficacy (that they can, are able to do this, in our globalized world).
… The **dynamism** of cities stands in stark **contrast** to the **increasingly dysfunctional** character of many national governments, which too often seem gripped by **paralysis**.…	His main thesis is to compare the positive virtues of cities (dynamism) with the increasingly dysfunctional national governments – gripped by paralysis.
Cities are **more nimble**, more attuned to the concerns of their citizens and **able to respond** quicker to their needs.	Whereas cities are more nimble (Efficacy), more attuned to citizens and 'able to **respond** quicker to their needs'.
In a world of fast-paced relentless change, cities **can cope better** with digital disruption **turning technological upheavals to their advantage**.	Cities can **cope** better with digital disruption and technological upheavals (which act to the advantage of cities).
Cities are also more **resilient** to economic shocks, as they **bounce back** faster.	They are also more **resilient**; a can-do attitude that reflects Efficacy.
… cities are **leading the way** and leaving central governments lagging behind."	In sum, cities are able to do what large central governments can't do; they 'lead the way'.
	All of this reads as a can-do Efficacy

Source: *The Economist.* The World in 2017. 'Maybe it's because I'm a Londoner', January 2017, p. 88. Permission to reprint granted by *The Economist.*

Figure 7.1 illustrates the three states, both in conflict and as a positive state.

Becoming more good humoured

We started this chapter with an anecdote about an immediate client who was quite morose. I was constantly being asked to 'lighten him up'. At that point we explored the People Model: the Life Conflicts model. We can see that this client would have Existence conflict (he was very low on Existence). He didn't appreciate new things, new ideas, new policies. In other words he didn't promote growth. He also had Elevation conflict by being selfish, dour and morose most of the time. He was the opposite of good humoured which is what his colleague was usually beseeching me to focus on. I remember watching him during a workshop and thought he was

124 *Life conflicts – individual*

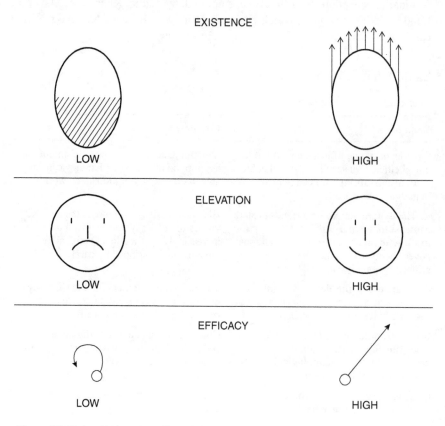

Figure 7.1 Three modes of conflict.

the most menacing person I had ever seen. Indeed, one day he started telling me about a vacation in Africa. I asked him what he spent his time doing and his answer was 'killing things'. I noticed the same look come over his face when he talked of making particular people redundant or firing them. Finally, he had a moderate degree of Efficacy because he believed in his ability to achieve goals.

Step three of the People Procedure: proportionate or equal

They had a proportionate one because the client was in control and intended to stay in control. In other words, he was in defensive mode.

Step four of the People Procedure: underlying needs and feelings

The feelings and needs underlying the three Life Conflict states are described in Table 7.2. In the case of my client, the dominant ones are feeling flat and dispirited as well as morose and selfish.

Life conflicts – individual 125

Table 7.2 How you feel in the presence or absence of life conflict

	Presence of life conflict	Absence of life conflict
Existence	Feel flat, dispirited, bored, shallow, meaningless	Feel fully alive, full of purpose, fresh and new, fulfilled
Elevation	Feel selfish, alone, morose, hopeless	Elevated, good humoured, feel as though you are not alone
Efficacy	Feel scared, chaotic, helpless, anxious	Feel things are smooth, feel confident, brave

Step five of the People Procedure: dominant theme

The dominant theme was his moroseness as part of Elevated conflict. This was the scary side of him and his effect was gloomy to most people who met him.

Step six of the People Procedure: did he want a solution?

Yes he did, once I had given him feedback in relation to the above.

Step seven of the People Procedure: resolution

He focused more on relationships and was more good humoured. But he still reacted with defensiveness to anything new.

Monitoring the three states

In order to illustrate each of the three states, I have diagnosed statements in terms of only one of those states. However, in practice you should be looking at all three. The need for this is demonstrated in the short section that follows and also in the case study at the end of this chapter on Steve Jobs.

I worked every so often as a consultant facilitator at a large Training Centre in the UK for about seven years. We were hired on a daily basis for about a few days every month. It was run and owned by a husband and wife team who were as different as chalk and cheese. Their profiles on the Life Conflicts Model are in Table 7.3.

Table 7.3 The husband and wife team

Husband's profile	Wife's profile
• Low Existence	• High Existence
• Very low Elevation	• High Elevation
• High Efficacy	• Low Efficacy

In some ways it looks as though they have chosen opposites. He was notorious at rejecting any proposal of newness that the consulting team suggested (low Existence). We had many disgruntled consultants as a result. She usually supported us but had only a nominal amount of actual power and authority.

126　*Life conflicts – individual*

He traded on us being Elated with clients, particularly as he had none of this attribute. He usually chose one of the consultants most high on Elevation to front up to the particular business group that week as a presenter. His wife was very high on this trait but was also low in Efficacy. He was very high on the latter and had the utmost confidence in his own abilities. However, he had a high turnover of staff and his wife ended up suicidal. All three states are implied in an overall pattern of performance and wellbeing.

What he never perceived was the importance of the first two states, Existence and Elevation, in running a business properly and well. He thought it was all down to self-confidence and ability.

Organizations and conflict

We can also decipher how the three states map on to the organization, not just the individual.

For Existence, a positive example is the small software companies in Cambridge Science Park in the UK. These employees want to lead a different life from the conventional one. They want to make quite a bit of money so they don't have to think about money. They want a meaningful existence.

The opposite occurred at London Business School where the atmosphere was flat. People did not really believe in what they were doing and some departments were not on top of the game in terms of ideas. They were successful but it was meaningless.

For Elevation, a group of very competent Sales Managers were positive examples. They always left me feeling on top of the world. For some, they were not as bright as their salesmen but the managers knew how to hire good and generous people.

The opposite is exemplified by most accountancy firms. They count pennies and lose pounds. They think motivation is about paying people more. In other words, they do not know what motivates people and are selfish.

As far as Efficacy is concerned, a positive example is a City insurance company which, while large, is entirely efficient and well-functioning. It sets very challenging goals and expects employees to meet them no matter what.

An example of poor Efficacy is the public sector. These organizations are the most dysfunctional of any I have been in either as an employee or as a consultant. They resist actually achieving anything. They can set goals, produce interminable pieces of paper but have very little impact. They can do a lot, very busily, but not accomplish much.

(The checklists at the back of this chapter can be filled out on an organization with respect to the three states.)

Conclusion

In this chapter, we have looked at a new concept or model which focused on conflict arising from the way you live your life. Each of the three states can be high or low as will be illustrated in the case study that follows.

In the next chapter, we explore some applications of the six models in the whole book.

Life conflicts – individual   127

Case study: Steve Jobs

Steve Jobs: the legendary ex-CEO of Apple Inc., had exceptional qualities as well as some notable weaknesses; all of which are thoroughly described by Walter Isaacson in his biography (2011). I have used that biography to describe Steve Job's personality in terms of the three Life Conflict states. The first dimension is Existence. In what follows in Commentary 7.4, I have placed quotes of Steve Jobs or Isaacson on the left-hand column with my commentary on the right-hand side.

Commentary 7.4 Steve Jobs: Existence

Steve Jobs – Existence	Commentary
"Your goal should be making something **you believe in** and making a company that will last" (p. 71)	This is what gives Steve Jobs a sense of meaning (Existence).
"We are **inventing** the **future**…. Think about surfing on the front edge of a wave. It's really **exhilarating**. Now think about dog-paddling at the tail end of that wave. It wouldn't be anywhere near as much fun. Come down here and **make a dent in the universe**" (Steve Jobs trying to recruit a programmer, p. 85)	This is his source of motivation: inventing the future. Exhilarating is an Existence feeling. Creating something new and doing something grand with your life is an Existence concept.
" 'It was like a veil being lifted from my eyes' Jobs recalled 'I could see what **the future of computing** was destined to be' " (p. 89)	Focusing on the future again.
"Steve was so **passionate** about building this amazing device that would **change the world**" (p. 105)	Being intense and passionate are (usually) Existence emotions. He wants to change the world.
"They [people Sculley brought in] cared about making money … rather than **making great products**" (p. 171)	This is **not** what Steve Jobs believes in: making money compared with making great products (Sculley was CEO of Apple for a time).

The second dimension is Elevation. Steve Job's weaknesses arise primarily in relation to Elevation; the positive personable state, focused on relationships. Commentary 7.5 illustrates.

128 *Life conflicts – individual*

Commentary 7.5 Steve Jobs: Elevation

Steve Jobs – Elevation	Commentary
"he could be charismatic, even mesmerizing, but also **cold and brutal**" (p. 59) "Wozniak began to rankle at Job's style. Steve was **too tough on people**" (p. 77)	For all Steve Job's strengths, he is described as 'cold' or 'brutal', 'too tough'; the exact opposite of the positive Elevated state.
"He could be very engaged with you in one moment, but **then very disengaged**. There was a side to him that was **frighteningly cold**" (p. 86) "As an executive, Jobs has sometimes been **petulant and harsh on subordinates** (p. 97; extract from a *The Times* article)	Being disengaged is also the opposite. This is the equivalent of 'cold and brutal'. There is a lack of generosity in this behaviour.
"At Apple his status revived. Instead of seeking ways to curtail Job's authority, Sculley gave him more…. He was flying high, but this did not serve to make him more mellow…. '**You guys failed**' he said, looking directly at those who had worked on the Lisa. '**You're a B team. B players. Too many people here are B or C players**' " (p. 167)	This is the brutal approach – telling people they are B or C players to their face, in public. (Note that Lisa was a computer.) No elevation or moral goodness here.

The third dimension is Efficacy. This shows up markedly when creating the iPhone. Commentary 7.6 illustrates.

Commentary 7.6 Steve Jobs: Efficacy

Steve Jobs – Efficacy	Commentary
" 'We all know this is the one [of the optional products] we want to do…. **So let's make it work**'. It was what he liked to call a bet-the-company moment" (p. 433)	Enthusing people that something is attainable is part of Efficacy. As Steve Jobs says, you just have to 'make it work'.
"Think of all the innovations we'd be able to adapt if we did the keyboard onscreen with software. **Let's bet on it and then we'll find a way to make it work**" (p. 433)	This is classic: we'll *find* a way to make it work, so high is the self-belief that they can achieve what they set out to achieve.
"[Wendell Weeks] tried to explain [to Jobs] that a false sense of confidence would not overcome … challenges, but that was a premise that Jobs had repeatedly shown he didn't accept. He stared at Weeks unblinking '**Yes, you can do it**,' he said. '**Get your mind around it. You can do it**' " (p. 435)	This is a statement of belief that you *can* get what you set out to.

Life conflicts – individual 129

Exercises

1 How do you make sense of the three states: Existence, Elevation and Efficacy?
2 Which of them do you feel most comfortable with and why?
3 Which of the following worries you the most: having no meaning in life; having no sense of being morally uplifted; or feeling unable to achieve what you want?
4 What can you do about your answer to 3 above?
5 How would you rate your organization in terms of Existence?
6 How would you rate your organization in terms of Elevation?
7 How would you rate your organization in terms of Efficacy?
8 If you were to develop your Existence state what would you do?
9 If you were to develop your Elevation state what would you do?
10 If you were to develop your Efficacy state what would you do?

Checklist 7.4 Existence in the organization

Rate your organization on a scale from 1 (low) to 7 (high).
Your organization:

Is unique, distinctive	1(low).............2.............3.............4.............5.............6.............7(high)
Loves new things	1(low).............2.............3.............4.............5.............6.............7(high)
Is creative	1(low).............2.............3.............4.............5.............6.............7(high)
Makes every moment count	1(low).............2.............3.............4.............5.............6.............7(high)
Feels fully alive	1(low).............2.............3.............4.............5.............6.............7(high)
Has a set of beliefs to live by	1(low).............2.............3.............4.............5.............6.............7(high)
Has a sense of meaning	1(low).............2.............3.............4.............5.............6.............7(high)

Total out of 49 =

---

130 *Life conflicts – individual*

Checklist 7.5 Elevation in the organization

Rate your organization on a scale from 1 (low) to 7 (high)
    Your organization:

Has a positive
nature   1(low)............2............3............4............5............6............7(high)

Likes doing the
right thing   1(low)............2............3............4............5............6............7(high)

Appreciates moral
goodness   1(low)............2............3............4............5............6............7(high)

Is generous   1(low)............2............3............4............5............6............7(high)

Good humoured   1(low)............2............3............4............5............6............7(high)

Likes doing things
for people   1(low)............2............3............4............5............6............7(high)

Focus on
relationships   1(low)............2............3............4............5............6............7(high)

Total out of 49 =

Life conflicts – individual   131

Checklist 7.6 Efficacy in the organization

Rate your organization on a scale of 1 (low) to 7 (high)
  Your organization:

Believes it can achieve what it sets out to	1(low)............2............3............4............5............6............7(high)
Sets high goals	1(low)............2............3............4............5............6............7(high)
Is efficient	1(low)............2............3............4............5............6............7(high)
Gets things done	1(low)............2............3............4............5............6............7(high)
Knows what is going on	1(low)............2............3............4............5............6............7(high)
Has deep not shallow confidence	1(low)............2............3............4............5............6............7(high)
Keeps momentum going	1(low)............2............3............4............5............6............7(high)

Total out of 49 =

Transcribe your scores to the table below:

Existence

Elevation

Efficacy

References

Algoe, S. B. and Haidt, J. (2009). Witnessing excellence in action: the other-praising emotions of elevation, gratitude and admiration. *Journal of Positive Psychology*, 4, 2, 105–125.

Bandura, A. (1977). Self-efficacy: toward a unifying theory of behavioral change. *Psychological Review*, 84, 2, 191–215.

Cox, K. S. (2010). Elevation predicts domain-specific volunteerism 3 months later. *Journal of Positive Psychology*, 5, 5, 333–341.

Frankl, V. E. (2000). *Man's search for ultimate meaning*. New York, NY. Basic Books.

Isaacson, W. (2011). *Steve Jobs*. London, UK. Abacus.

Seligman, M. E. P. (2002). *Authentic happiness*. New York, NY. Atria Paperback.

8 Applying the People Models

Getting an overview
So far, we have explored six People Models and ranged over different components of the organization. We started with conflict in inter-organizational relationships, moved to the organizational (structure and team), the interpersonal and individual levels. We know we can use every People Model at any of these, even though I have illustrated their use in only one chapter at a time as we went through the book. At this point, we apply the People Models like a pick and mix – as you would in practice. We need to choose one which makes sense of the issues or person at hand and, also, one which we have a rapport with. In actual fact, my favourites to use are the two I created; the Partner–Ally–Friend model and the Life Conflicts one. In spite of this, in what follows I use mostly the Partner–Ally–Friend model, the Myers Briggs Type Indicator (MBTI) and the Inclusion–Control–Openness model as they related most easily to the particular people and situations I analyse.

Somehow, we need to streamline the process of applying the People Models. This chapter is aimed at showing you some ways to do that. It is the case that the words in various statements or utterances can be different but the People Model analysis stays the same. This is because you are looking below the surface level.

We start by examining a few issues you can look for; the sort of things organizations and the people in them fall victim to. Then we explore four politicians: Obama, Clinton, Trump and Blair, focusing on Trump. They might all be politicians but they are poles apart on the People Models.

Key points in this chapter
Key points in this chapter are set out in Table 8.1.

Table 8.1 Key points in this chapter

- Getting an overview
- Key points in this chapter
- Culturally preferred styles
- Applying a procedure
- Applying the People Models: politicians
- Barack Obama
- Hillary Clinton
- President Trump
- ESTP
- Tony Blair
- Conclusion

Culturally preferred styles

When I am trying to understand a situation of conflict in an organization or an individual, I will start by becoming aware of the available data rather than guessing what they might be on the People Models. In this chapter, we will be scanning and reading books instead of real live people or organizations since to do the latter is impossible in this context.

The next step will be to be aware of the presence of culturally preferred styles as reflected in Table 8.2.

All of these biases form the seed-bed of conflict. That is because they usually lead to imperialistic behaviour – whether of an organization or an individual. Another source of resolution of conflict, then, is to balance the divergent functions or dimensions in any context. (This does not mean equalize them.) This takes a developmental perspective as well as tolerance for differences.

Some of the cultural biases are evident in what follows.

Cultural biases: Thinking not Feeling

With the MBTI (Chapter 3) as well as the Jungian model (Chapter 6), in most organizations there is a bias towards Thinking and away from Feeling. This difference is not real but due to cultural pressure. You can see this emphasis in organizational statements of any description. My favourite is looking at advertisements of MBA programmes or Executive Education courses. (This interest is because I worked at London Business School for four years.) These are almost wholly focused on the Thinking function and not the Feeling function. (I have seen ads that are 95 per cent Thinking and 5 per cent Feeling.) What does this mean? For Feeling types this situation is full of conflict. It might mean that they are alienated. That there is no connection between them and the business school. What happens to values and ethics in the school (something Feeling types are particularly interested in)? What happens to the post-bureaucratic organizations, quite a few of which are Feeling based?

In reality, what is the actual percentage of Feeling to Thinking types? In the US, 44 per cent of men and 76 per cent of women report they are Feeling types (Myers *et al.*, 1998, p. 157). What, then, are the Marketing Departments doing other than being out-of-date and too macho? They are projecting a fantasy of hero-managers without 'getting' that Feeling types are supremely competent as well.

Table 8.2 Culturally preferred styles in the Western world

Culturally preferred	People Model involved
Ally	Partner–Ally–Friend model (Ch. 2)
Extraversion, Thinking	Myers Briggs Type Indicator (MBTI) (Ch. 3)
Control dimension, Boss	Inclusion–Control–Openness model (Ch. 4)
Action (man manager)	Gestalt Cycle of Experience model (Ch. 5)
Ego	Jungian psychic model (Ch. 6)
Efficacy	Life Conflicts model (Ch. 7)

134   *Applying the People Models*

Boss not Juggler

Another obvious trait of organizations and individuals is in the Inclusion–Control–Openness model (Chapter 4). Here we have a bias towards the Control dimension (as compared with the Inclusion or Openness dimensions). Even more, the Control nature that is displayed or required more often than not is the Boss and not the Juggler. Both want to win; they do so with a different control style. Bosses use power and Jugglers use agility. Both want to be empowered but Jugglers want to empower others. 'Power', 'battle', 'sharpening your leadership skills', 'strong' are all Boss words or phrases. To reach a Juggler audience you have to refer to releasing talent, working at speed, being adventurous and so forth. I have often had clients that were struggling to reduce a Boss nature or enhance a Juggler one. Conflict arises because, in practice, organizations and individuals are trying to move from a Boss mode to a Juggler mode or to keep a Juggler mode but our long-standing out-of-awareness cultural bias prevents us.

Other biases

Other biases with respect to conflict to look out for in practice are being an Ally not a Friend on the Partner–Ally–Friend relationship model. The bias in the Gestalt Cycle of Experience model is to take Action(s): to be an Action Man manager and ignore the requirement for Mobilization and Contact. There is much inner conflict arising from a bias towards responding to the ego rather than the Self. Finally, it is to focus on Efficacy rather than, say, Elevation or Existence in the Life Conflicts model. The implication of the latter is that the individual or organization may be excellent at self-belief and have confidence in their competence but don't have the attributes of good humour (Elevation) or the attributes of innovating (Existence), both of which are needed to decrease individual life conflict.

Applying a procedure

The following steps can aid you in putting the People Models to use in understanding and working with conflict. The most important is the first one. Without this, all the other steps are irrelevant.

- Be completely open to the data.
- Read/scan different parts of the book/article/individual behaviour or organization action to see what the conflict is about.
- Monitor for cultural bias. If the person or situation are 'imperialistic', look for ways to illustrate that their way is only one way, not the only way. This is the crux of resolving conflict.
- *Wait* till an obvious interpretation *forms* in your mind. Don't impose a pre-formed interpretation.

Applying the People Models 135

- Keep reading/scanning/listening until you get an idea which People Model to use to understand the conflict.
- If no interpretation emerges, consider (a) whether they are a politician or a political organization, (b) are they an extreme Professional? With either of these, it will be very difficult to analyse them (see Obama and Clinton).
- While you keep reading/scanning/listening, take note of what is emerging in your diagnosis.
- Once you are sure of your diagnosis on one model, see if any other People Models help you to interpret.
- Consider the timing of the diagnosis (as per Tony Blair).
- Consider the context the person or organization is in. Is the organization or person behaving appropriately for that context?

Applying the People Models: politicians

The focus of this chapter is to use the People Models to analyse well-known politicians; this enables us all to know who we are talking about. It means we will be using the models at the individual level rather than the organizational level. However, this is the level that can most easily be used to learn to apply them anyway. There are four politicians: ex-President Barack Obama, ex-US Secretary of State Hilary Clinton, President Donald Trump and ex-British Prime Minister Tony Blair. Their personalities are maximally divergent, I think!

Barack Obama

The key points with Obama are:

- His manner of speech is sometimes to negate what he is saying (hence you can't analyse it).
- He seems to be a Professional by implication (see Chapter 4).
- The word-crafting is so extreme his personality can sometimes not be seen.
- He does focus almost exclusively on one aspect of the People Procedure, being equal, which is the core principle to reduce or remove conflict.

There were two books I used to analyse him. The first was a book of his speeches (Dionne and Reid, 2017) and the second a favourable biography (Chait, 2017). "A remarkably substantial number of critics and saddened supporters alike have described Obama and his era as a time of unfulfilled promise, poetry without prose" (Chait, 2017, p. xvii). This sentiment is partly because of his way with words.

Negating what he is saying, psychologically

Negating what he is saying makes his speech uninterpretable in terms of People Models. Here is one example:

136 *Applying the People Models*

"Hope is *not blind optimism*" Obama said early in his campaign, "It's *not ignoring* the enormity of the task ahead or the roadblocks that stand in our path. It's *not sitting* on the side-lines or *shirking* from a fight. Hope is that thing inside us that insists, *despite all the evidence to the contrary*, that something better awaits us if we have the courage to reach for it and to fight for it."

(Dionne and Reid, 2017, p. xviii, my emphasis)

He is talking about 'hope' but, in spite of the connection to Elevation in the Life Conflicts model, you cannot conclude that his speech is about Elevation. His negations cancel this out. His sentiment, that Hope will dispel conflict, would hardly be realized with this text.

Professional

Obama seems to be a Professional not an Attractor (Chapter 4). An Attractor is high in Openness and the Professional is low. The latter are careful how they are seen by others. He is probably a Professional because of the latter and is difficult to analyse with the People Models. Much of what he says is very crafted. He is trying to be all things to all people. For example, the following speech is about his decision to run for President. My commentary focuses on which one of the three dimensions of the Inclusion–Control–Openness model applies to his speech. This is a confused speech, if analysed psychologically, or with a People Model. If looked at superficially, without thought, it is a clever mix of platitudes. It is, therefore, a speech of a very strong Professional. Commentary 8.1 illustrates.

People Procedure

Obama's speeches are, in spite of my earlier comments, aimed frequently at reducing conflict. As a politician, Obama talks a great deal about treating everyone as *an equal*. This, in itself, is good. It is not an aspect of a People

Commentary 8.1 Extract from Obama's speeches

Extract from Dionne and Reid, 2017	*Commentary*
"**I chose to run for President** at this moment in **history**	Control dimension/Openness
because I believe **deeply** that we cannot **solve the**	Openness/Control
challenges of our time unless we **solve them together**,	Control/Inclusion
unless we **perfect** our **union**, by understanding that we	Control/Inclusion
may have **different stories**, but we have **common hopes**	Inclusion/Openness
... we all want to move in a **common direction**: toward	Inclusion/Control
a better future for our **children and our grandchildren**"	Openness
(p. 53)	

Applying the People Models   137

Model but is a core step in the People Procedure (see Chapter 1). The following quotes illustrate what I mean.

> "There's not a black America and white America and Latino America and Asian America" he said, "there's the United States of America."
>
> (Chait, 2017, p. 2)

> My friends, we have not come this far as a people and a nation because we believe that we're better off simply fending for ourselves. We are here because we believe that all men are created equal, and that we are all connected to each other as one people.
>
> (Dionne and Reid, 2017, p. 18)

> We are one people, all of us pledging allegiance to the stars and stripes.
>
> (Dionne and Reid, 2017, p. 12)

> the moral certainties we now take for granted – that separate can never be equal, that the blessings of liberty enshrined in our constitution belong to all of us.
>
> (Dionne and Reid, 2017, p. 16)

This principle, of equality, I described in Chapter 1 as being of fundamental importance to decreasing conflict. So, to choose this is a useful step. It even, probably, defines his Presidency; helped him get elected. It does not, however, negate the evidence that he is difficult to analyse.

Hillary Clinton

For Clinton, I have used her autobiography (Clinton, 2014) as the source of data. For the most part, Clinton seems to be, like Obama, a Professional – so strong she is also difficult to analyse. However, it is possible to depict a style of Partner, rather than an Ally or Friend, in terms of the People Model in Chapter 2. This is particularly clear when she is describing her international activities. In the following extract from her autobiography, I have contrasted her words with those of Aung San Suu Kyi (Myanmar leader) who is a Friend on the Partner–Ally–Friend model. (Clinton is advising Aung San Suu Kyi on how she should behave, now, as a leader.)

> You have to figure out a way to *keep working together* until or unless there is an *alternative* path. This is all part of politics. You're *on a stage* now. You're not locked away under house arrest. So, you've got to *project many different interests and roles all at once* … now she had to *learn to wheel and deal* like any elected official.
>
> (Clinton, 2014, p. 111; my emphasis; dialogue occurs in September 2012)

138 *Applying the People Models*

Aung San Suu Kyi, for her part, says in a subsequent speech:

> I stand here now in the knowledge that *I'm among friends* who will be *with us* as *we* continue with *our* task of *building a nation*.... There will be difficulties in the way ahead, but I am confident that *we shall be able to overcome all obstacles with the help and support of our friends.*
>
> (Clinton, 2014, p. 112; my emphasis)

So, here we have an example of a distinct Partner and a distinct Friend. Could this lead to conflict? It depends on the maturity of the two involved. It could lead to disagreements but not necessarily conflict if they saw the other person as different but equal. Conflict would arise if they saw the other person as different and wrong.

Gobbledygook

Aside from the references to a Partner mode, most of what Clinton writes is almost impossible to interpret with the People Models. One tiny example is as follows: "I told them [everyone who had campaigned and voted for me] I believed in public service and would remain committed to helping people solve their problems and live their dreams" (p. 6).

While worthy, it is still gobbledygook.

One story she tells, about preparing her speech to support Obama, runs like this.

> I wanted to strike the right balance between respecting my voters' support and looking toward the future. In person and over the phone, *I went back and forth with speechwriters and advisers seeking the right tone and language.* Jim Kennedy ... had woken up in the middle of the night thinking about how the 18 million people who had voted for me had each added a hole in the ultimate glass ceiling. That gave me something to build on. I didn't want to repeat the standard bromides; this endorsement [of Obama] had to be *in my own words*, a convincing personal argument.
>
> (Clinton, 2014, p. 5, my emphasis)

How can it be 'in her own words' when she is going back and forth with speechwriters and advisers?

This is part of that speech:

> I addressed the disappointment of my supporters directly. Although we weren't able to shatter that highest, hardest, glass ceiling, it got about 18 million cracks in it. And the light is shining through like never before, filling us all with the hope and the sure knowledge that the path will be a little easier next time.
>
> (Clinton, 2014, p. 6)

Applying the People Models 139

This isn't 'in my own words'. What does this mean for conflict, when a person tries to be all things to all people? It would still lead to conflict because that person isn't being real. Aside from that, gobbledygook is virtually impossible to analyse with the People Models.

President Trump

Unlike Obama and Clinton, Trump's personality is not papered over; not manicured to appear perfect. With Donald Trump, we have a personality bursting at its seams, to a fault. Every one of the People Models can be populated by him – unlike Obama and Clinton whose personality was aimed at appearing politically correct. However, whenever I mentioned to my colleagues or friends that I was analysing Trump, the news was greeted with derision. Why was this the case?

The only biography of him that I read was acidic in its views (D'Antonio, 2016) so I read three of Trump's books as well (Trump, 1987, 2004, 2015). These conveyed his personality in spades.

He appears to be an Ally, in the Partner–Ally–Friend model (due to his forceful approach to other organizations and countries). He appears to be an Extraverted, Sensing, Thinking, Perceiving type on the MBTI. He seems to be a Populist, Boss, Attractor on the Inclusion–Control–Openness model. He has quite a functional profile on the Gestalt Cycle of Experience except he interrupts the cycle with diversions about his accomplishments; he appears, in his role as President, to be pressured or required to move away from the Ego position to more of a Self position. Finally, he focuses on Efficacy first followed by Elevation and lastly Existence in the Life Conflicts model. In what follows I analyse only the first three profiles (Chapters 2 to 4). The other dimensions and models can easily be discerned in his writing and speaking.

Context

The context that needs to be explained refers to three relevant facts:

- He was a very successful property developer.
- He *did* win, over Hillary Clinton.
- As President he is very unpopular.

Partner–Ally–Friend

The model easiest to apply to President Trump is the Partner–Ally–Friend (Chapter 2). This framework focuses on the relationship assumed and desired with other organizations or people. To analyse this I have concentrated on his 2015 book and its reference to the USA's place in the world. The relationship type he describes is that of an Ally, with barely a trace of the Partner or Friend. Commentary 8.2 illustrates.

140   *Applying the People Models*

Commentary 8.2 Trump: the Ally

Trump's Partner–Ally–Friend	Commentary
"America needs to start winning again.... Yet ... everybody is eating our lunch. That's not winning" (Trump, 2015, p. 1)	The Ally is full of force and bravado. They interact with others with the intent of 'winning'. They do not like being a loser.
"And when we try to negotiate with foreign countries? We don't stand up. We don't threaten to walk away. And, more importantly, we don't walk away. We make concession after concession. That's not winning" (Trump, 2015, p. 1)	Not walking away from foreign countries is 'not winning'.
"And I will have Mexico pay for that wall. Mark my words ... one way or another, they are going to pay for it" (Trump, 2015, p. 20)	This quote, with Mexico paying for the wall, is also revealing the forceful side of the Ally. Note the phrase 'I will have', 'Mark my words' and 'one way or another'. He wants his own way.

The Ally is very strong. No doubt it would be useful, in the role of President, not property developer, to develop some of the Partner or the Friend or both because of the complexity of the issues in that role.

The second analysis is that of his MBTI. This highlights (as is usual with the MBTI), his strengths. (Refer to Chapter 3.)

Myers Briggs Type Indicator (MBTI)

Trump's MBTI seems to be that of an ESTP. That is, an Extravert rather than an Introvert, a Sensing type rather than an Intuitive (with qualifications), a Thinking type rather than a Feeling type (with qualifications) and a Perceiving type rather than a Judging type. This profile may or may not lead to conflict depending on the maturity of the person in dealing with others. Whether or not it happens will partly be a function of whether the person tries to 'balance out' their functions.

Extraversion and Introversion

Trump does try to deliberately balance out Extraversion with Introversion. He seems to be, however, primarily an Extravert. Commentary 8.3 illustrates.

Conflict is more prevalent when a person has excess Extraversion or Introversion. What is the evidence that this is so with Trump? One worrying feature is his proneness to approve of people who are like himself (boundless energy and motivated – in other words, Extraverts). Here is an example where a clear Introvert is not chosen to work with:

"But what I discovered very quickly is that Meier is not the sort of guy who jumps in with great energy and enthusiasm. He spends time pondering and theorizing" (Trump, 1987, p. 338). It is hard to imagine Trump working with direct reports where they are strong Introverts. They might be seen as 'wrong' not 'different'. His extraversion might, then, be a source of conflict. Table 8.3 illustrates.

Applying the People Models 141

Commentary 8.3 Trump on Extraversion: Introversion

Trump's Extraversion: Introversion	*Commentary*
"I happen to enjoy giving speeches ... I get so much energy from my audiences that it is always fun" (Trump, 2004, p. 61)	This is not an Introvert being described. It would be unusual for an Introvert to like giving speeches that much. An Extravert gets energy from doing them. Is his Extraversion extreme? Probably.
"It made me realise how much I need a certain amount of quiet time – usually about three hours a day – in order to stay balanced. It's time I use to read and reflect, and I always feel renewed and refreshed by this. It also gives me material to feed my extraverted nature" (Trump, 2004, p. 91)	Here he refers to his Extraverted nature. We know he deliberately balances out his extreme Extraversion with Introverted activity. While it is, developmentally, a good sign that he takes an Introvert-break, it is not necessarily enough to 'balance' him especially if he is strongly Extravert. He might need to alter his Introversion activity so that, instead of reading a lot of journals and newspapers (which satisfies his Extraversion), he reads fewer and more in depth (which would satisfy his Introversion).

Table 8.3 Stable and excess Extraversion and Introversion

E excess	*E stable*	*I stable*	*I excess*
Boundless need for attention	Moderate need for attention	Good at keeping boundaries	Too hidden
Exaggerates	Easily copes with presentations	Calm	Loathes presentations
Talks too much	Likes to talk	Thinks before speaks	Too shy

Sensing and Intuition

The quotes in Commentary 8.4 illustrate that Trump is likely to be more of a Sensing type than an Intuitive. Commentary 8.4 illustrates.

Thinking and Feeling

Trump seems to be clearly a Thinking type but there is, in his 2015 book, a trace of the Feeling function. The Thinking function on its own is clear in Commentary 8.5.

The Thinking function running the White House seems to be repeating some of his property-developer formulae for success: aim high, keep pushing. Conflict will arise, however, from an adversarial Thinking. It is so blunt. He certainly could have some Feeling function to soften out the Thinking. All the remaining quotes in this next section (Thinking and Feeling) come from his 2015 book, released during the US elections. They are, then, more about America than property development.

Trump's Sensing: Intuition	*Commentary*
"The contractor who's building my pool at Mar-a-Lago is on the phone…. We're going to great lengths to build a pool in keeping with the original design of the house, and I want to make sure every detail is right" (Trump, 1987, p. 25)	Making sure every detail is correct is a constant theme for him. It is associated with Sensing.
"I'm a very practical guy" (Trump, 1987, p. 35)	As is being 'practical'.
"Some people have a sense of the market and some people don't. I like to think I have that instinct. That's why I don't hire a lot of number-crunchers, and I don't trust fancy marketing surveys. I do my own surveys and draw my own conclusions" (Trump, 1987, p. 51)	Not trusting number crunchers or fancy marketing surveys sounds like a distrust of Intuition.
"All is going well, but every detail is important and there are a lot of them to take care of" (Trump, 2004, p. 174) "Elaine and I troubleshoot the latest detail" (Trump, 2004, p. 199)	Here are the details again.
"The real reason I wanted out of my father's business … was that I had loftier dreams and visions" (Trump, 1987, p. 79)	However, there is also some intuition. Trump appears to be a bit of both, with the Sensing stronger. Intuition has the loftier dreams.
"If you see the entire planet as an emerging market – which it is – you'll discover that you've got a lot of homework to do every day" (Trump, 2004, p. 177)	It is also the capacity to see the invisible future. In other words, Trump seems to be both Sensing and Intuition, with the former appearing to be stronger. My own instinct is that he does both in concert with each other, rather than cancelling each other out (either can happen). My reasoning for this is that his success as a property developer would almost certainly be impossible unless Sensing and Intuition work together.
"[The USA] needs someone with common sense and business acumen" (Trump, 2015, p. xi) "What [America] needs is … to apply practical solutions" (Trump, 2015, p. xiv)	In his book written in 2015, campaigning for President, he does, however, seem only a Sensing type (common sense and practical solutions). There is less sign of Intuition. Without it, there might be conflict from people/organizations needing the larger picture not just practical solutions.

Applying the People Models 143

Commentary 8.5 Trump on Thinking: Feeling

Trump's Thinking: Feeling	Commentary
"But I won't let my personal judgment affect my business judgement" (Trump, 1987, p. 12)	Personal judgement sounds like Feeling and business judgement sounds like Thinking.
"My style of deal-making is quite simple and straightforward. I aim very high and then just keep pushing and pushing and pushing to get what I'm after" (Trump, 1987, p. 45)	Pushing and pushing sounds like Thinking.
"I try not to [equivocate]. Fortunately, I don't have to try too hard at this one because I've been known to be on the blunt (and fast) side at times" (Trump, 2004, p. 15)	He does, however, equivocate as is seen in another section following. Being blunt is being Thinking more than Feeling.
"Still, sometimes you've just got to screw them back" (Trump, 2004, p. 139) "Screaming at them is what I have to do" (Trump, 2004, p. 169)	Screwing them back and screaming at them is an adversarial Thinking function.
"I call an employee at a large property who has not been as attentive as his position demands. I tell him that his bad performance is not his fault, but mine. I simply hired the wrong person by overestimating his capabilities. I add that if he'd like to change my mind about my initial mistake, it's up to him" (Trump, 2004, p. 190)	Here is the Thinking function's emphasis on performance.

In what follows I concentrate on one part of his 2015 book that deals with the media: What is the answer? Does the media love him or hate him? It is a highly confusing message. In what follows I have picked out parts of a passage which demonstrate Feeling or Thinking (alternating). Commentary 8.6 illustrates.

Commentary 8.6 Trump on the media

Trump on the media	Commentary
"There are many reporters whom I have a lot of **respect** for" (p. 10)	Feeling
"**I don't mind being attacked.** I use the media the way the media uses me – to attract attention" (p. 10)	Thinking
"Recently, I was interviewed by … Hugh Hewitt. – Every question Hugh asked me was like [**Trivial Pursuit**].… In the end, though, Hugh Hewitt was just **fine and has since said some great things** about me. Everything was '**gotcha, gotcha, gotcha**'. Truthfully, though, I can't **really blame** Hugh Hewitt for doing what he did … he figured out the best way to get attention is to **attack Donald Trump**" (pp. 15–17)	Thinking Feeling Thinking Thinking Thinking

144 *Applying the People Models*

Commentary 8.7 Trump on Judging: Perceiving

Trump's Judging: Perceiving	Commentary
"Most people are surprised by the way I work. I play it very loose.... You can't be imaginative or entrepreneurial if you've got too much structure. I prefer to come in to work each day and see what develops" (Trump, 1987, p. 1) "But what the hell? I'll wing it and things will work out" (Trump, 1987, p. 13)	Trump might seem unpredictable and chaotic to those around him. He would if, for example, he were surrounded by people who assume that organizing and managing in a Judging way is the correct and only way to do things. It isn't. In my experience, Perceiving types have the capacity to get more things done. Nevertheless, in spite of my sympathies to a Perceiving type, the safest solution is to develop some Judging while fending off those around him as much as possible.
"I know how to deal with complex issues and how to bring together all the various elements necessary for success" (Trump, 2015, p. xiv)	Knowing how to deal with complex issues etc. is Perceiving.

Aside from anything else, this mix of alternating Thinking and Feeling is bewildering. It isn't an integrated position but one where they cancel each other out. It makes him look a bit stupid and shows that he prevaricates. I think the truth in Commentary 8.6 is encapsulated in an end-position of Thinking being still dominant. If he is developing his Feeling function, which is a great idea, he needs to do it faster. While he is developing it, it will appear more chaotic and touchy than when fully developed. This dimension is probably partly responsible for the degree of conflict that emanates from the White House. More Feeling would modify that conflict.

Judging and Perceiving

Trump appears to be a clear Perceiving type as shown in Commentary 8.7.

ESTP

In aggregate, then, Trump would seem to be an ESTP. This, in temperament theory (a variant of type theory) (see Myers *et al.*, 2009, p. 60), is described as an Artisan (for SPs alone). Their description reads as:

> The Artisan's core needs are to have the freedom to act without hindrance and to see a marked result from action. Artisans highly value aesthetics whether in nature or in art. Their energies are focused on skilful performance, variety and stimulation. They tend toward pragmatic, utilitarian actions with a focus on technique. They trust their impulses and have a drive to action. The Artisan's learning style is often concrete, random and experiential. Artisans enjoy hands-on applied learning with a fast pace and freedom to explore. They tend to be gifted at employing the available means to accomplish an end.

Applying the People Models 145

(Note that this is (as per usual) written solely from the position of strengths and preferences.)

The ESTP is one of 16 types, all of which are equal. The advantages of any one type derive from the maturity with which one uses it. Note that his dominant would be ES (Extraverted Sensing).

In summary, in the MBTI, Trump might evoke conflict primarily through any strong Extraversion, an adversarial Thinking function and a quite marked Perceiving attitude. All of these may need to be restrained a little, partly by balancing them with their opposites, Introversion, Feeling and Judging. The conflict can be lessened by an approach that others, with a different MBTI profile, are equal to the ESTP. Extraversion can be helped by increased Introversion activity; Sensing combined with a little Intuition is probably a strength for him; the Feeling function can be developed more; and the Perceiving attitude is not wrong but, in the interests of harmony, could compromise a little with the Judging attitude that is probably around him.

Trump: Inclusion–Control–Openness model

The Inclusion–Control–Openness model is not so starkly obvious for Trump as the Ally or the MBTI we have just looked at. In this model, there are three dimensions: Inclusion which relates to general interaction with others, needing attention and staking out one's territory and existence. Control relates to issues of power, control, authority, competence, speed and size. Openness relates to issues of relationships and intimacy and how open you are vis-à-vis others. In order to elaborate the meaning of these three dimensions I have created a word to describe the ends of each dimension (see Chapter 4). The inclusion dimension contains a Connoisseur (low in Inclusion needs) and a Populist (high in Inclusion needs). The Control dimension contains a Juggler (low in control needs) and a Boss (high in control needs). Finally, the Openness dimension contains a Professional (low in openness) and an Attractor (high in Openness needs). On these dimensions President Trump would appear to be a Populist, Boss and Attractor.

Commentary 8.8 illustrates the suggested profile.

President Trump is a strong advocate of each position. He appeals to the masses (Populist) and seeks publicity. He likes to be completely in control (Boss) and in charge. He puts himself in the leadership position of cleaning up America. Finally, he is a strong Attractor which his supporters would recognize (saying things as they are).

Tony Blair

One of the important factors to be aware of in applying the People Models is any changes that occur across *time* and the increase or decrease in inner conflict that ensues. This is the case with ex-British Prime Minister, Tony Blair. Another

146 *Applying the People Models*

Commentary 8.8 Trump – Populist, Boss, Attractor

Trump as Populist	Commentary
"I use the media the way the media uses me – to attract attention. If you do things a little differently, if you say outrageous things and fight back, they love you. So sometimes you make outrageous comments" (Trump, 2015, p. 10)	The desire for attention is typical Populist even to the point of making 'outrageous' comments.
"But there's nobody like me. Nobody" (Trump, 2015, p. 74) "Nobody can build a wall like me" (Trump, 2015, p. 23)	Calling attention to yourself is also the Populist. There is some exaggeration in these two comments. Nobody like me. Nobody can build a wall like me. This is an extreme position – extreme Populist?

Trump as Boss	Commentary
"This mess calls for leadership in the worst way" (Trump, 2015, p. xi) "I told [a rally] that we need a military so strong that we don't have to use it" (Trump, 2015, p. 3)	These quotes are so transparently Boss they barely need commenting on. A Juggler wouldn't refer to high control solutions (such as the military).

Trump as Attractor	Commentary
"I say what's on my mind" (Trump, 2015, p. 7) "We don't have time to pretend" (Trump, 2015, p. 8) "What I say is what I say" (Trump, 2015, p. 9)	Pinpointing him as an Attractor is somewhat counter-intuitive. However, recall that an Attractor is high in Openness. Therefore, they say what is on their mind. He doesn't have time to 'pretend' (which is how a Professional will appear to him). The Attractor is one of the main reasons he won the election.

important factor is to take into account the *context* for your interpretation and whether or not there is a fit between the environment and the response. If there isn't a fit, the conflict will get worse.

I have used two books to understand the ex-Prime Minster; first, his auto-biography (Blair, 2010) of his very good display of the Professional and Attractor, and the second is Bower (2016).

The Professional is one aspect of the Openness dimension (see Chapter 4). It is low in Openness which means people 'present' themselves, like to appear professional, but choose to not be open about what they are feeling or who they really are.

The Attractor is the opposite. Their preference is to be high in Openness. They tend to reveal themselves comfortably, are OK with emotion and are more self-expressive.

Applying the People Models 147

The dynamic across time of the Attractor and Professional

Tony Blair expresses both the Professional and the Attractor in what follows. To note is the way that both are expressed initially in his first fight to become Prime Minister, but, in his final election and from then on, the Professional has taken over. (He seems to be naturally an Attractor so there is an amount of inner conflict that emerges over time.) Commentary 8.9 illustrates (using quotes from Blair, 2010).

Commentary 8.9 Tony Blair's Professional and Attractor

Tony Blair's Professional and Attractor	*Commentary*
"I strode to the polling station with Cherie and the children, the ideal family picture ... **smile, but not exuberantly. Talk, but not with too much animation**" (p. 3)	This is amusing. He, as an Attractor, 'watches' or 'monitors' the Professional. The Attractor says 'smile' and the Professional says 'not too exuberantly'.
"Everyone [is celebrating] except for me, that is, my predominant feeling was **fear**" (p. 1) "the root of my fear [was that] I was **alone**" (p. 11)	Here he is describing winning a landslide election. The Attractor was aware of the emotion of fear while others are celebrating. At base, he is 'alone'.
"**But I put my best face on**" (p. 11)	And here is the Professional putting his 'best face on'.
"I was about to **blow my top** when I decided to use **icy calm** instead. **More prime ministerial**" (p. 295)	The Attractor wants to blow his top but instead he opts for the Professional route, icy calm.
"And here is a real political lesson. You have to '**feel it**' to succeed in politics" (p. 305)	Feeling it, as he puts it, is the Attractor.
"We knew we have twelve hours ... and we had to **have a line** by then.... I **personally** felt the thing was extraordinarily **funny**" (p. 323)	In this hilarious episode he recounts his reactions after the incident where the Deputy PM punched a member of the public. The Professional goes for 'the line' they have to have but the Attractor behind the scenes finds it very funny.
"The trick, actually, is to **appear to be natural**, while **gripping your nature in a vice** of care and caution. **Don't let the mask slip**" (p. 344)	By now he is switching more to the Professional. He says the trick is to 'appear' to be natural, not 'to be natural'. This is the Professional cloaking the Attractor. The Professional is 'gripping your nature'. The mask is the Professional.
"In this time, I was trying to wear what was effectively a kind of **psychological armour** which the arrows simply bounced off" (p. 573) "And the key to surviving was to **keep your head**" (p. 589)	Psychological armour is the Professional. Survival is from being the Professional; keeping your head.

continued

148   *Applying the People Models*

Commentary 8.9 Continued

Tony Blair's Professional and Attractor	Commentary
"I had always been known as the politician with the **sure touch**, the one who could express the public's thoughts and, therefore, shape them.… They [Parliamentary Labour Party loyalists] felt I had **lost this ability**; and with it, what **made me who I was**" (p. 602)	Here he talks of the Attractor giving way to the Professional in the eyes of others. He had, apparently, 'lost that sure touch with the public'.
"[The public and Tony Blair] were like two people standing either side of a **thick pane of glass trying to have a conversation**" (p. 658)	A thick pane of glass between two sets of people trying to have a conversation is the Professional.
"I communicated and **felt normal at the beginning** and then over time seemed to **become distant, aloof, presidential**.… The predominant view, however, was that I had lost that common touch" (p. 658)	He feels normal at the beginning of his reign as Prime Minister (Attractor) and then later feels like a Professional (distant, aloof).
"The farewells had to be gone through, with dignity … but **without mawkishness** … no point in anything other than try to **take one's leave decently**" (p. 661)	Mawkishness is a word said to any Attractor left in him so it knows to not get in the way and be 'emotional'. Things must be 'decent' instead, i.e. the Professional.

Has Tony Blair altered his personality so he is now a Professional while he used to be an Attractor? I don't think so. I think he is, by nature, an Attractor but the Professional took precedence (maybe only for a while?). Where is the conflict? First, there is inner conflict between the Attractor and the Professional. Second, there may be Life Conflict in that his trademark Elevation might not be so apparent. Third, there is Interpersonal conflict with members of the Parliamentary Labour Party coming to see him to point out he had lost the common touch. What is the resolution? To bring back some of the Attractor and leave it in charge.

Taking context into account: Blair and his response to the Chilcot report

Another important factor to take into account when using the People Models is the context or the environment. The latter can be characterized with a People Model. In what follows I have quoted from Bower (2016). I am staying with the Inclusion–Control–Openness People Model to analyse this because it can build on the analysis already done.

Table 8.4 sets out the conflict when the actual response given is different in nature from the response required. It means that one is using a dimension which is inappropriate.

Applying the People Models 149

Table 8.4 Conflict arising from an inappropriate response

Inappropriate words or action	Result
Inclusion instead of Control	Can be incompetent in order to get attention
Inclusion instead of Openness	Really superficial relationships
Control instead of Inclusion	Power behind the throne
Control instead of Openness	Harsh and 'clipped'
Openness instead of Inclusion	Relationships too deep and unnecessary
Openness instead of Control	Never achieving anything

The context for Tony Blair and the Chilcot report is that the public and the media want the truth revealed. This situation is, therefore, defined by Openness. However, the Control dimension takes over. In other words, the context needs an Openness response and gets a Control one.

In what follows, Control words are in bold. Openness words in the form of the Attractor are underlined, and Openness words in the form of the Professional are italicized.

Tony Blair addressed the media after Sir John Chilcot's report had been published. (This was a British public inquiry into the nation's role in the Iraq war, published in July 2016.) Commentary 8.10 illustrates.

Did these words make the situation better or worse? They certainly would have made it better if the public and the media were on the receiving end of more of an Openness response.

Commentary 8.10 Blair and the Chilcot inquiry

Bower's Biography of Tony Blair	Commentary
"In a croaking voice, he portrayed himself as a '**decision maker**' and accepted '**full responsibility without exception** and **without excuses** [for] the **hardest** most momentous and most agonising **decision** I took in my ten years as British Prime Minister…. For all this I express more *sorrow, regret and apology than you will ever know or can believe*'…. While accepting **responsibility** for the **decision** to remove the **Iraqi leader**, he rejected **blame** for the bloodshed that subsequently erupted across the world: 'What **I can't do** and will not do is say that we took a **wrong decision** … I didn't mislead this country" (p. 595)	It is clear that the control dimension gets most of the emphasis. When the situation is dealt with by a different psychological nature, it is likely to get worse (Control for Openness). Note that the Professional takes over control of the Attractor in the middle of his statement by stating 'more than you will ever know'. That is the Professional in control of the Attractor who would want to refer to sorrow regret and apology rather than tell people they would never know about it. In spite of this, the Professional and Attractor are roughly equal.

150 *Applying the People Models*

Conclusion

In this chapter we have explored different sources of conflict and the People Models that deciphered them. The first section looked at cultural bias which can lead to imperialistic behaviours. The bulk of the chapter explored four leading politicians in view of the People Models. Both Obama and Clinton seemed to speak too much in gobbledygook. They illustrated how it can be impossible to get 'underneath' their speech to the person there. Trump and Blair were, in some ways, the opposite and quite easy to read.

Exercises

1 What are the biases in the different People Models that lead to imperialistic behaviours?
2 How do you know these biases are present?
3 Are you speaking or writing gobbledygook (is your organization)?
4 How do you know?
5 Do you speak or write in a self-negating fashion?
6 Can you apply the six models to the people in your organization?
7 Can you apply them to your organization as a whole?
8 What are your sources of conflict over time, say ten years?
9 Are you too excessive in any of the People Models?
10 Do you match your responses to the context or environment (in People Model terms)?

References

Blair, T. (2010). *A journey*. London, UK. Arrow Books.
Bower, T. (2016). *Broken vows*. London, UK. Faber & Faber.
Chait, J. (2017). *Audacity*. New York, NY. Harper Collins Publisher.
Clinton, H. R. (2014). *Hard choices*. New York, NY. Simon & Schuster.
D'Antonio, M. (2016). *The truth about Trump*. New York, NY. Thomas Dunne Books.
Dionne, E. J. and Reid, J. A. (2017). *We are the change we seek: the speeches of Barack Obama*. New York, NY. Bloomsbury Publishing plc.
Myers, I. B., McCaulley, M. H., Quenk, N. L. and Hammer, A. C. (2009). *MBTI manual*, 3rd edn. Mountain View, CA. CPP Inc.
Trump, D. T. (1987). *Trump: the art of the deal*. London, UK. Arrow Books.
Trump, D. T. (2004). *How to get rich*. London, UK. BBC Books.
Trump, D. T. (2015). *Crippled America: how to make America great again*. New York, NY. Simon & Schuster.

Index

Page numbers in **bold** denote tables, those in *italics* denote figures.

acquisition(s) 1, 18
Action 12, 84, **85**, 87
Administration and Marketing departments
9–10, 35–40
Ally 13, 16–17, 20–21, **22**, 24–30, 27, **27**,
29, 31–32, 139–140
angels 4–5, **5**
applications 13, 132
Attractor 65–66, **65**, *66*, 69, 71, 74,
145–150
Awareness 12, 84, **85**, 87

Bailyn, L. 5
balance between conscious and
unconscious *100*, 101–103
Bandura, A. 117
bargaining conflict 45–48
Beckhard, D. 5, 92
black holes 55
Blair, T. 12, 132, 145–150
Boss 63–65, **64**, *65*, 70, 73, 134, 145–146
Branson, R. 30, 112
bullying 2, 106
bureaucratic conflict 41–45
burnout 103–106
business model(s) 1, 2
business procedure 9–11, **9**, 15

Cambridge Science Park 18
Chilcot report 148–150
Clinton, H. 12, 132, 137–139
computer users groups 16
conflict 1–4, **5**, 6, 12, **13**, 148, **149**;
bargaining 45–48; Blair 148; between
Partner, Ally, Friend 21–22;
bureaucratic 41–45; computer users
groups 16; cultural preferences 133;

efficacy 122, *124*, **125**; elevation 120,
124, **125**; existential 118, *124*, **125**;
functional or lateral 34–40; inner 98–99;
Interpersonal **80**, 82, 89; job excitement
19; life conflicts 117; meta-theoretical
traditions 7, **7**; team 55, 58, **61**, 62–63;
Trump 140, 144–145; values 14;
voluntary sector 23–24
confluence 80–81
Connoisseur 63–64, **63**, *64*, 69, 72
consulting 1, 34
Contact 12, 84–85, **85**, 87–88
Control 12–15, 58–62, **59**, **61**, **62**, 64, *65*,
67, **67**, 76, 134, 145, 150
cultural biases 133, **133**

defence mechanisms 79–82
Deflecting 80, **81**
demons 4–5, **5**
development profile 114
dominant 37–38

Efficacy 12, 121–123, 128, 131
Elevation 12, 120–121, 128, 130–131
empowered leadership 86
enantiadromia 105–106
ESTP 144
evocative mode of influence 89–92, **89**
executive committee 56–67
Existence 12, 117–119, 127–129, 131
Extraversion 36–37, **37**, 40, 42, 51, 53,
140–141
Extravert 37–40, **38**, **39**, **42**, 46, **46**, **101**,
102, 140

Feeling 36–40, **37**, **38**, **39**, **42**, 43, 47, **46**,
49, 52, 133, 141–144

152   *Index*

Ferguson, Sir Alex 12, 29, 69–71
Flight Centre 12, 93–94
Frankl, V. 12, 117–118
Friend 13, 20–24, **22**, 26–27, **27**, 29

Gestalt model 2, 13
Gestalt Cycle of Experience 12, 82, 84–85, 95–96
gobbledygook 139
good humoured 123–124

Haidt, J. 12, 117, 120
HR annihilation 45–48

Inclusion 57–58, **61**, 62, **62**, 67, **67**, 68–69, 75, **149**
Inclusion–Control–Openness model 2, 12–13, 57–68, 134, 145, 148
individuation 110–111
inner conflict 98, 145
Introversion 36, **37**, 39, 42, 51, 53, 140–141
Introvert 36, 38, **38**, **39**, 40, **42**, **46**, 47
Introverted Feeling types 108–109, **110**
Intuition 36, **37**, 38, **38**, 39, **39**, 42, **46**, 49, 51–53, **101**, 141–142
Intuitive 38, **38**, 39, **39**, 40, 42, **42**, **44**

Jobs, S. 12, 127–128
Judging 37, **37**, 38, **38**, 39, **39**, 40, **42**, 43, **44**, **46**, 47, 49, 52–53, 144–145
Juggler 63–64, **64**, 65, *65*, 73
Jung, C. 2, 12–13, 99–108

Khan, S. **116**, 123
Koestlebaum, P. 86

Life Conflicts model 2, 12–13, **13**, 117, *124*

May, T. 12, 49
merger in the public sector 25–28
mergers 1
Merkel, A. 12, 29
MIT 2, 5, 79, 92
Mobilization 12, 84–86, **85**
Moon J. 116, **116**, 121
Myers Briggs Type Indicator 2, 12, **13**, 35–49

Negotiating to Yes 24–25
Nevis, E. 2, 5, 12, 79, 81, 89–92

Nutmeg 99, 107

Obama, B. 12, 132, **132**, 135–137
Openness 57, 59, **59**, **61**, 62, **62**, 65, 66, *66*, 67, **67**, 68, 77

Partner 20–27, **27**, 30
Partner–Ally–Friend model 2, 10, 13, **13**, 17, **17**, 20–27, **27**, 31–32
People models 4–6, 8, 10–12, **13**
People Procedure 3–4, 8–11, **27**; applied to the acquisition 19–23; public sector 25–28; retail Company 41–45; annihilating HR 46–48; Executive Committee 56–62; Swiss Alps 82–86; Cat 99–105; boss' protégée 106–108; life conflicts 117, 123–125
Perceiving 37, **37**, 38, **38**, 39, **39**, 40, 43–44, **42**, **44**, **46**, 52–53, 144–146
Pondy, L. 34, 41, 45
Populist 63, **63**, *64*, 69, 72, 145–150
Professional 65, **65**, *66*, 69, 74, 136–137, 145–150
projecting 79, **81**
Provocative mode of influence 89–92, **89**

relationships 1
resistance to the Cycle of Experience 85, **85**
resistances to change 45–46
resolution 9, **9**, 10, 85, **85**, 86, 88–89
retail company 41–45
Retroflection 81–82, **81**

Schein, E. 5
Schutz, W. 2, 12, 57
Sensing 1, 35, 36, 37, **37**, 38, **38**, 39, **39**, 40, 42, **42**, 43, **44**, **46**, 47, 49, 51–53, 140–141
simulation 83–86
Swiss Alps 82–86

teams **13**, 55, 57–59, 62
Thinking 36, 37, **37**, 38, **38**, 39, **39**, **42**, 43, **46**, 47, 49, 52–53, 133, **133**, 141, 143–144
Trump, D. 2, 12, 132, **132**, 139–145

values 13–14
voluntary sector 23–24

Wojcicki, S. 116, **116**, 119